LONDON IS A PLACE

LONDON IS A PLACE

DOMINE DIRIGE NOS

Leonard Feeney

BOSTON
THE RAVENGATE PRESS
MCMLI

Also by Leonard Feeney:

IN TOWNS AND LITTLE TOWNS

THE BROWN DERBY

RIDDLE AND REVERIE

FISH ON FRIDAY

GOSPEL RHYMES (joint author)

BOUNDARIES

SONG FOR A LISTENER

YOU'D BETTER COME QUIETLY

THE ARK AND THE ALPHABET (joint author)

THE LEONARD FEENEY OMNIBUS

YOUR SECOND CHILDHOOD

MOTHER SETON

THE CHILDREN

AND OTHERS.

TABLE OF CONTENTS

The coat of arms on the title page is that of the City of London. The shields at the head of each chapter are respectively those of: Sir Thomas Malory, St. Thomas More, William Shakespeare, John Milton, John Dryden, Percy Bysshe Shelley, Thomas Babington Macaulay, and Alfred Lord Tennyson.

LONDON IS A PLACE

I

THE FOG

London is a place. Berlin is an idea. Paris is both a place and an idea. London could never be a different place, but it could readily be a different idea. London is not a geometrical but a geographical center, around which additions are made not by way of logic but of land.

London is the fixed center of something for which no circumference, or shape of any kind has been found. Take out your map of the world. Observe the spaces which are blotted out in red. You will then see the utterly shapeless, yet completely factual thing of which London is the center.

All distance is measured from London, whether it be in practical science (longitude, East and West), or in practical sentiment ("Come down to Kew in lilac-time; it isn't far from London!").

London is the temporal city, temporal in the full sense of time as our senses report it. Rome is eternal. Paris is perpetual. Berlin is recurrent. But London is continual.

All time is reckoned from London (Greenwich), and sounded from it (Big Ben). If you want to set your watch in any part of the world, you must refer to London time. And London time is not any logical standard, but an otherwise capricious clock, regulated by London, and preserved in one of its observatories.

If you want to know the distance from one place to another, you must turn to London's standard of distance: a metal bar, arbitrarily called "a yard" and hidden in the House of Parliament.

Paris measurements are in the beautiful metric system, and are made in terms of a logical standard, because Paris is both a place and an idea. Paris calls one ten millionth of one quarter of the earth's circumference a meter; and with ten as a logical standard of numeration, a cube as a logical standard of shape, and water as a natural standard of weight, Paris constructs logical norms: for volume, in terms of a liter; for weight, in terms of a gram. London measurements are of an entirely different kind.

What happens to be the local unit in London, is expected to be the standard unit everywhere. A rod is 16½ feet. Why such a queer number of feet? Because it happens to be the length of something in London. A mile is 5280 feet. Why the 280? Because it happens to be the distance from someplace to someplace in London. 2000 pounds make a ton. Why? Because that is what something in London weighs, when you put it on something else, arbitrarily called "a scales."

London is not the place you go to learn anything. It is the place you go to observe. London is not only full of observatories and museums, it is itself both a museum and an observatory.

London is neither right nor wrong, true or false. London is correct. And scrupulously precise. London never dismisses anything false by saying: "It couldn't be done!" London never dismisses anything wrong by saying: "It shouldn't be done!" London merely says: "It isn't done!", by which is meant: It isn't done in London.

London is not only spatial and temporal, it is completely local. London does not mean England. London does not even mean Britain. England is a lot (a good deal) of land protected by water. Britain is a lot of (a great many) lands protected by ships. But London is a lot (a plot) of land protected by both.

Liverpool may be the port of departure from London to the rest of the world, but London itself is always the point of that departure. For the essence of a *locus,* in so far as it can have one, is seen in the point of departure. When a Londoner retires to the country for a vacation, he refers to this as living *in* the country. He also refers to it as living *out of* London. London is the place a Londoner lives "out of" when he lives "in" any other place, be it Ottawa, Calcutta, or Rangoon.

You never become a Londoner by going there to live. You do not even become a Londoner by having come to life there. For London is more than a space and a place: it is a place within a space, a section within a section. It is, in a word, *a spot*. And the specifications for *the spot* have been correctly inked in the London code.

If you have been born in the wrong part of London; or if you have been born in some other city: Manchester, Birmingham, Sheffield, Bristol (unless your birth there can be explained as an accident, as some sort of visit, for which you had official permission), it is already too late to become a Londoner. London can use you—from the wrong town, the wrong district, the wrong cradle—it may even adopt you (legally), but it will never elevate you to the status of *the spot*.

The passport to being a Londoner is not your birthright (which could spot you anywhere), but your birth certificate (which puts you on the spot). If everything comes off as specified—if you are Tommy Twicklethorpe III, grandson of Thomas Twicklethorpe II, born of wealthy and idle (or at

14

least bankrupt and indolent) parents, and entitled to something either in land or litigation the instant you begin to breathe at No. 2 Tottenham Terrace; if, in a word, you are "the time, the place, and the loved one all together," then, and only then, are you a Londoner. And once stamped with the London seal of approval, you may become as cosmopolitan as you care to. You cannot be corrected in any other part of the world even though you go to Turkey and wear a fez. You *are* correct.

Besides being spatial, local, temporal, precise, and correct, London is (and no wonder!) thoroughly material. London gives nothing cultural, racial, social, or religious, to any of its far-flung towns, whether it be Belfast, Baghdad, or Bombay. London merely regulates what it finds there. In return for its laws, it demands their loyalties. It never takes any culture from its subservient cities, only their cargoes.

Mr. Masefield, London's present poet laureate, acknowledges that the ancient quinquireme of Nineveh brought culture in its cargo from distant Ophir to sunny Palestine:

With a cargo of ivory,
And apes and peacocks,
Sandalwood, cedarwood, and sweet white wine.

Likewise, Mr. Masefield agrees that the medieval galleon brought culture as well as cargo back from the Isthmus, through the Tropics, to Spain:

With a cargo of diamonds,
Emeralds, amethysts,
Topazes, and cinnamon, and gold moidores.

But, on Mr. Masefield's own admission, here is what comes back to London from its disparate dependencies:

Dirty British coaster with a salt-caked smoke stack,
Butting through the Channel in the mad March days,
With a cargo of Tyne coal,
Road-rail, pig-lead,
Firewood, iron-ware, and cheap tin trays.

And what does London dispense to its dominated areas in return for this raw material? Mr. Kipling, Mr. Masefield's unofficial predecessor, has already told us. It is:

Boots—boots—boots—boots, movin' up an'
    down again!
There's no discharge in the war!

A cargo of dragoons and discipline (English dragoons and London discipline), that's what goes *out* from London by way of boats.

Oh, of course, London has a merchant marine, as well as a fleet of warships, and it would not be true to say that London sends them back always empty to the ports from which they came. But they carry, on their return voyage, no produce, only products. "Give us the materials, and we will make the things!" has ever been London's commercial cry on the sea. "Give us the money, and we will make the investments!". . . "Give us the territories, and we will make the treaties!". . . "Give us the weapons, and we will win the wars!". . .

Now the essence of matter, according to the philosophers, is found in this: in a material thing that asks for nothing but what is material, and gives nothing material back. Such a thing is London.

Or, is it a thing? Outsiders refer to London as a noun: "London hears . . . London feels . . . London regrets . . . London demands . . ." Insiders refer to it as a pronoun: "We feel . . . We maintain . . . We demand . . . We are determined . . ." One does not know in just what category of *thingness* to place London. Is it a site, or a set? A set-up, or a sentiment? One will never know, in an entity so undefinable. Whatever it *is,* history reports something it once *had.* It once *had* a local nationality (English), and a universal religion (Catholic). It now *has* a local religion (Anglican), and a universal nationality (British). London is the temporal, material, local pivot around which this weird rotation was made. That is why I call it a place. Not an idea. And certainly not a place and an idea together.

If you become surfeited with what London offers you by way of place, and would like to enjoy what Christendom offers you by way of abode, London never refers to this as "going over to Catholicism."

It always refers to it as "going over to Rome." London feels that a change of faith, or even a change to Faith, is a change of local allegiance. London can keep you terribly frightened about making this change, and terribly worried after you have made it, by the incessant use, with the sibilant stressed, of a single word: "disloyal."

I have said that London is continual. How does it continue? Where does the new London come from when the old one disappears? The answer is that there is never a new London, only the old one continued. A "New London" could appear only in the United States, and that would not be the place, only the name.

But where do the new Londoners come from when the old ones die? Again a foolish question. For there are never any new Londoners, only the old ones repeated. You become a Londoner, not in a lifetime, but in a minute. You are just as much a Londoner when you are Tommy Twicklethorpe III drinking milk in your crib, as when you are Tommy Twicklethorpe II drinking whiskey in your club.

The children of London live in London. The children of Londoners do not. The children of Londoners live outside the city in private institutions known as "public schools." The children of London stay in London, play in the streets, starve in the slums.

When the children of London grow up, they become, not Londoners, but the people of London. And they still play a game they used to play in the streets: *London Bridge is falling down!* In the air raids of modern war, the Londoners either leave the city, or are hidden under it. But the people of London stay in the streets. *London Bridge is falling down, falling down on you!,* O people of London, fortunate to be even the ruins of such an irreplaceable area.

London is a pleasant place for poets to live in. Not profound poets, of which London has none, but pleasant ones. London once had a profound poet, Shakespeare, but he was a profound funeral oration on the spiritual death of England: "To be, or not to be!" London had another profound poet, Milton, but he was a profound memorial service: "Paradise Lost." Since then, London has had no profound poets, only pleasant ones, and perhaps more pleasant ones than any other city in the world.

It is pleasant for the poet to refer to refreshment as "cakes and ale," instead of just calling it "food." It is pleasant for the poet to refer to time as "Big Ben," to recreation as "Kensington," to music as "Covent Garden," to punishment as "Coventry," to torture as "The Tower," even to usury as "The Old Lady of Threadneedle Street." London is just the right concretion for the small ideas that small poets get. It supplies them with pleasant names for unpleasant things, and with even more pleasant names for the pleasant ones. It is no wonder that the greatest small poet London ever had (Charles Dickens) dispensed his poetic localisms in prose. For prose is the best medium for setting small standards for other writers to copy: Scrooge, Mr. Pickwick, Mr. Murdstone, Mr. Pecksniff, Peggotty, Uriah Heep. Whenever London had on its hands anything larger than a small poet, he either became a pantheist, and therefore too unlocal for London; a transcendentalist, and disappeared into China by way of opium; or else a man with a good honest heartache, who ran off to the Continent and was buried in Rome or drowned on the shores of Greece.

In music London has Gilbert (a poet) chasing Sullivan (a composer) up and down the scale and trying to match every note of a Londonderry air with the syllable of a London word.

Left all to itself as sheer matter (for matter, after all, exists, and is therefore beautiful) London is, on a quiet evening, or an almost-sunny afternoon, dotted with small tokens of its own typical and topical beauty. I knew, when I visited London some years ago, that I would find the right person and place to represent it, and that I would find them together.

I found them in the person (and place) of a dear old man, sitting on one of the benches in Bird Cage Walk, just outside the important precincts of Buckingham Palace. No one could call this man "John Bull." But it would be easy and graceful to call him "John O'London."

This old man is the quintessence of everything lovely and local in London, as Dickens was wont to describe it. He is memorable, indispensable, unique. He is not in the least "out of his mind," but there are some things he does not seem quite able to remember.

John O'London does not circulate through the Empire as Londoners do. He sits on the same bench, day after day, year after year, decade after decade, with birds about him, his head full of dreams, a book in his hand, and a sprig of lavender in his coat. He remains, and almost *is* London.

In status, this lovely old man is half way up from the slums, half way down from the gentry. He is gentle, without the right to be called, there, "a gentleman." His voice is quiet and refined. His language is choice, without being "educated." His hair is a beautiful English silver (foggy silver), and his eyes are a beautiful English blue (springtime blue).

Old John O'London (elderly, would be a better word than old) knows all the important things that are happening in politics, and all the select things that are happening in social circles. But he himself is neither political nor select. He is reserved.

His courtesy to a duke is as effortless as his kindness to a beggar. His is that spirit out of which everything lovely and local in English literature has been molded, molded in the most beautiful local language (I believe) in the world.

One both likes (likes terribly) and pities (pities terribly) this exquisite old man, too innocent to know how good he is, too stupid to know what he represents.

One thing I noticed about him particularly. He is never, never, never in a hurry. He has altogether too much time on his hands.

II

SKYSHINE

So much for London as a material fact. Now let us look at it as a moral entity.

Here the fog lifts, melts into a mist. The source of brightness is not yet seen. But one knows that the sun is shining. There are signatures of light behind that almost perpetual veil of clouds in which London is wrapped. This condition of weather (London's most usual weather) I have heard Londonites refer to as "skyshine."

Londonites! Where did I get that name? Perhaps it is a name that is used, perhaps it is a name I invented. In either case, I am going to let it stand. Because I need it. I need it so as to group together both the Londoners and the people of London in an amalgamated moral program, the tenacity and durability

23

of which I believe to be unequalled in any other city of this earth. Material London is the philosopher's despair; and if any philosopher, by means of those correct but imperfect standards of thought known as "abstractions," can solve London as a cosmological riddle better than I did in the last chapter, he is welcome to the assignment; and I am willing to see myself corrected in terms of his logical appraisement, but not in terms of his patriotic or political abuse.

When I finished the first chapter of this essay, called "The Fog," I read it aloud to a group of London loyalists. They winced at almost every paragraph. When I finished reading, they remarked, almost with one voice: "Oh, come now! There's much more to London than that!" And I agree with them. There's always much more to anything than the philosopher alone sees, particularly when he sees it through a fog. The philosopher's logic is the blueprint of the edifice of thought. But it is not the finished building. And no amount of logic, divorced from the arts and insights of love and leisure, will turn it into a home.

I know, and everyone knows, that the picture of London which I have drawn in the last chapter is not a charitable one, in the sense of being a painting, or even a photograph. It is rather a clinical picture, an X-ray film (a foggy thing at best), showing not what London looks like, but what it is suffering from. Let me now turn from an examination of London's material weakness to an appreciation of its marvelous moral strength.

London is, beyond all question, the most moral city in the world. I do not mean the most virtuous, for virtue is something more than mere moral performance. It is moral to be patient, moral to be obedient, moral to be pure. But there are times when a situation calls not for patience, but for indignation. The Victorians were not virtuous, but they were obedient. The Puritans were not virtuous, but they were pure.

Morality established by traditional practice, meekly accepted and stubbornly observed, is not virtue, but it sends off little shoots and flowers of character that so nearly resemble virtue that it is hard to distinguish them from it. Such traits as tidiness, neatness, promptness, accuracy, politeness, submissiveness, cheerfulness, thoroughness, reliability—one will not find these asceticisms expressly prescribed in the statutes of ethics or moral theology, but they are the characteristic behavior of nearly all Londonites. Such expressions as: "Cheerio! . . . Chins up, lads! . . . Let's not whimper! . . . Don't show the white feather! . . . Attend to your business! . . . All hands on deck! . . . Mind your manners! . . . Take off your hat to the lady! . . . Look before you leap! . . . Too many cooks spoil the broth! . . . There'll be bluebirds over the white cliffs of Dover, tomorrow, just you wait and see!" These are hardly the ethical or religious exhortations one expects to find in Plato's *Republic,* St. Thomas More's *Utopia,* or St. Augustine's *City of God;* but they are the kind of civic slogans one hears uttered and re-uttered, charmingly and cheerfully, year after year, in the Temporal City that lies on the Thames. And if my reader thinks I have not found it fascinating to be in the midst of such a moral milieu, surrounded by eight million well-disciplined people, so predictably patient, obedient, thrifty, prompt, cheerful, plucky and reliable, then he will have to explain why I lingered in London for weeks, walked in its streets, listened to its conversation, dined in its mansions and hovels, and always felt myself in the presence of something undeniably and unexplainably precious. What is right with the London moralism, I know. What is wrong with the London morality, it will take a little time to discover.

London morality is built up almost entirely on a few basic and generic observances. Be loyal! Be decent! Be careful! Be economical! Be contented! Be respectable! Be cheerful! Be sporting! Play the game!

Play what game?

Let us look at the game of loyalty, first, as it is played in London by the poor, including paupers and prostitutes; second, as it is played by the privileged, including politicians and princes.

From here on I have no desire to be clever, only

to be fair. And if what I say is not fair, let it be put down to a shortage of Londonism in my own character.

Let us go into the London slums, and sit at the table of a pauper, and see what difficulties we encounter in trying to teach him the beatitude of Christian poverty. The blessedness of Evangelical poverty we could never explain to a London pauper, unless he found his destitution unfair, insufferable, unjust. Were he to find it so, and were he to resent it with every energy of his soul, we could then show him how to endure it, with the aid of Grace and the comfort of Christ, Who, for love of us, became the poorest of the poor.

But the astounding—and I am bound to say—admirable feature of the London pauper is that he does *not* resent his poverty, and does *not* find it unbearable. He has schooled himself to cope with it entirely on his own resources: a courageous eye, through which cheerfulness shines as through a film of cloud; and a ready smile, that displays a row of soiled and disordered teeth. The London pauper does not love his deprivations (no one could), but he *is* loyal to them: even in the form of dinginess, dirt, disease and the dole. Nor is it by mere animal courage that he achieves this allegiance. It is by some sort of semi-mystical, but definitely spiritual will-power, that makes him want to remain part of what Gerard Manley Hopkins refers to as "Commonweal":

. . . *Commonweal*
Little I reck ho! lacklevel in, if all had bread.

The London pauper does have bread, thank God. But what kind of bread it is, I leave it to the dieticians to declare.

The case of the London prostitute is even more puzzling. In the guise of respectability, without anything of romance or much of remuneration, she goes street-roaming without remorse or regret. Let us call her to the bar of conscience (symbolized by a constable, a clergyman, or a court inquisitor), and see how she makes her report. It would go something like this, with all the h's unaspirated:

I met him on the bridge, serjeant (or "your reverence," or "my lord"). It was long after dark, and I didn't have the best of intentions. In fact, I expect the whole business was pretty much my fault. . . .

I asked him what time he retired for the evenin'. He said: "Oh, about ten o'clock, usually." I told him it wasn't my custom to retire quite so early. . . .

"And what do you do stayin' up so late?" said he. "Oh, this and that," said I. . . .

We stood chattin' till it was well on to midnight. It was a damp, cold night, and I expect we were both a bit lonely. . . .

The landlady heard us comin' into my room.

But she's the decent kind, an' didn't say nothin';
though I know she could hardly approve of
what was goin' on. . . .

I walked back with him to the train, at two
o'clock in the mornin'. He had to catch a train
at that time, because he was leavin' next day for
India on a boat. . . .

He was really a nice sort, and not nearly as
wicked as I drove him to be. . . .

"Good luck, lad!" I said to him when we
parted. "Good luck to you, wherever you go! I
expect you'll try to forget me in a hurry, and it
doesn't matter. I'm not the decent kind, as you
jolly well found out. But some day you will meet
a proper girl; and when you do, you don't even
need to mention that you met me. . . ."

That's about all, serjeant. I had to be up the
same mornin' at six, because the landlady is not
well, and I likes to help her with the breakfast. . . .

This cheerful unchastity, this feminine chivalry,
this impure pluck, may seem, at first blush, appeal-
ing. But it is not. It is appalling.

The red-light districts of London wear the same
color of lampshade as the areas of respectability.
And this is puzzling. And it is not good.

Now, let us go over to London's fashionable section, and visit one of the politicians.

"Politician" is not a good name for him technically, for only in a limited number of cases is he elected to office by the votes of constituents. He is nearly always appointed to office by someone higher up. He is usually the secretary, or sub-secretary, to someone who, in turn, is secretary, or sub-secretary, to someone else. I call him "politician" in preference to "government official," "government agent," or "diplomat," because the word covers the extreme politesse with which he manages both his government's domestic difficulties and his government's foreign affairs.

Wherever you meet the London politician, whether it be in nearby Downing Street or distant Dakar, his technique is always the same. Unlike the American politician, you never encounter him in a disgusting room, full of cigar smoke, littered with over-stuffed waste baskets and badly-aimed-at spittoons. The London politician always receives you in a formal and conservatively arranged office, seated at a neatly tidied desk, with the portrait of somebody's ancestors hanging behind him on the wall. And when you finally get in to see him (past the various secretaries and sub-secretaries who have tried so urbanely to discourage the visit), you never have an audience with the London politician, as you might with the Pope. He always has an audience with you. The American politician is all mouth. But the London politician is all ears.

He is a marvelous listener. As long as you do not
ask the London politician to talk, he will give you,
for the stipulated time of your visit (fifteen minutes
at the most) what seems to be (and may well be, for
all I know) his undistracted attention. He will
rarely offer you a solution of the difficulty about
which you came to consult him; but he will invari-
ably be full of sympathy . . . full of understanding
. . . appreciative of just how you feel . . . most
anxious to see if something cannot be done.

He will not, of course, make you any promises.
But he will take down your name and address, and
will write them slowly and deliberately on a piece
of paper. And when he dismisses you, exactly at the
end of the fifteen minutes he agreed to give you, if
you leave his office with the same grievance you went
in with, you will at least have added to it a glow that
makes it for the moment bearable. For you will
have undergone the exhilarating experience of never
having been listened to so uninterruptedly in your
life. And you will also remember how courteously
the London politician, at one point in your excitement, when you were at a loss for a word, supplied
you with the word, the very word you were looking
for, right out of Roget's *Thesaurus*.

What delightful manners, what quiet repose, and
easy reserve, go with the vocation of being *always*
sympathetic, *always* understanding, *always* anxious
to help, *always* deeply aware, *always* non-commit-

tal, and *always* full of regrets, no one can fail to see.
And if you add to this political recipe: a good tailor,
a good club, good food, and often extremely good
looks, you will understand why the London politician
is the most irresistible political agent in the universe.
Even the Sudanese, the Siamese, the Senegalese,
girded with loin cloths, with spears in their hands
and rings in their noses, sense his quality: a quality
of sustained and unimpeachable loyalty, loyalty to
the London scheme of things, which is one of the mir-
acles of moral observance in this messy and perfid-
ious world.

One last word about the London politician. He
will rarely make a speech. Speeches are too revealing. But he loves to make a report: a confidential
report, bristling with little shy disclaimers such as:
"to the best of my knowledge," "as far as I can observe," "if my judgment may be trusted in the matter."

Don't you worry, Mr. London Politician, your
judgment *will* be trusted. For if there are any facts
lying around the world which are to London's advantage, you will find them, ferret them out, even
though you have to go on holding conferences with
this one and that one till the clocks run down and
all the pages are torn from the calendar. The Temporal City knows it can rely on you, knows that you
will never let it down. And if this be not loyalty, then

to paraphrase a phrase of Patrick Henry, it's up to the rest of us to "make the most of it."

For our last study of a typical Londonite, let us call on an aristocrat. Incidentally, I want a real aristocrat, not a spurious one. For this reason, I shall studiously avoid paying my respects to those very recent peers, Sir So-and-So and Lady This-and-That, who lately blossomed among the nobility, not by the route of blood, but by the route of bigger and better biscuits for the Empire.

I am also anxious, in my quest for an aristocrat, to steer clear of a Lord, for fear of meeting a member of the House of Lords, true aristocrats, to be sure, but somewhat strait-laced, political and uncomfortable, from having always to vote the way the House of Commons thinks they ought to.

Our best bet, therefore, among the aristocrats, will be a Duke, a genuine, genealogical, honest-to-goodness Duke, who inherited his title from his father, and who loyally loiters in London year in and year out, by way of being more on exhibition than anything else.

The Duke at whose door we knock is neither the most dignified, nor the most discreet, of the European titularies. Indeed, there is almost no resemblance between him and what would be called a Duke in any country on the Continent. But he is the most lovable old good-for-nothing that ever could be.

33

The Duke is delightfully informal. He hates to dress for dinner. He hates to wear those various decorations he received for not fighting in the memorable battles that Britain won. The Duke despises all pretense, all fuss, all bother. As if to discipline him in these vagaries, Providence has surrounded him with a retinue of servants, so rigid and severe, as to be positively terrifying, even to the Duke. The Duke is constantly wanting to do things which his butler forbids with a censorious clearing of the throat, which his valet vetoes with a frown. Even the housekeeper has the Duke well in hand, and frequently dares to administer him a scolding. The Duke's wife, the Duchess, is usually in league with these higher servants, whose sole function seems to be to put the Duke in his place. It is only among the menials of his household that the Duke may let down, and be his dear old lovable and unpretentious self. The Duke gets along famously with the gardener, the charwoman, the boy who cleans his boots.

Besides being terrorized domestically, the Duke inflicts terror abroad. He is the especial terror of newspaper men and politicians. The news reporters almost never interview him in one of London's political crises, because the Duke is likely to say the impulsive and totally wrong thing. Such statements as, "Damn it all! why don't we let Gandhi out of jail? . . . Damn it all! the Pope is the only man in the

34

world who sees this situation clearly! . . . Damn it all! why don't we give the people a picnic or a parade? . . . The American girls are a pretty lot, don't you think so? Damn it all!"

The newspaper reporters never hear these remarks. And never, never offer them as copy to their various journals. It wouldn't be the London thing to do, to "take advantage of the Duke" in one of his explosions of temper.

The London politician has even a harder time with His Highness, the Duke.

Shhhhhhhhhh!................

"But do you think, sir, that would be the wise thing to say just at this moment? . . ."

"I know very well, sir, but you must remember there are other angles to the case which we must all endeavour to appreciate. . . ."

"We are doing everything in our power, sir, to see to it that the people get better living quarters, and just as soon as this present crisis is over, you will see, I trust, sir, the fruits of our efforts. . . ."

"But that's because you don't know the people of Australia, sir. . . ."

"But that's because you've never been in Canada, sir. . . ."

"But that's because the Irish are such an impetuous lot, sir. . . ."

"But that is the fault of the Indians themselves, sir. . . ."

Shhhhhhhhhhhhhhhhhhhh!. . . . .

But there are certain territories where the Duke will not be either deterred or hushed up. He will not be deterred from patting a newsboy on the head and paying him sixpence for a penny paper. He will not be deterred from going to the funeral of a dead tobacconist who was wont to supply him with his favorite pipe mixture. He will not be deterred from inviting Pobbles, the professional (not amateur) cricket player to dinner, and asking him to give exhibitions of his wrist-strokes in the middle of the living room. Nor will he be hushed up in calling his misdemeanors the names which properly apply to them: "I made a fool of myself! . . . I took far too much whiskey. I was completely potted! . . . I would never have got home if the cab driver hadn't helped me to find my own house. A good lad! Married, and has six children, so he told me. I gave him three pounds, which was all the money I had on me, and told him to distribute them among his children. I'll bet they're damn good-looking children, too, with not nearly enough to eat!"

There was once a London king, who, fantastic as it may seem, had dreams and desires of becoming a duke.

Aristocratically the thing made no sense.

Ethically it was totally reprehensible.

Religiously it was an outrage.

But as an exhibition of person-to-person loyalty, if we may detach the trait from every suitable prop that is needed to give it support, it was one of the most marvelous exhibitions of moral courage of this generation.

"At long last . . ." the alarmed Londonites heard him say one day over the wireless. And some of their eyes loyally filled with tears when he came to the unforgettable phrase: "for the sake of the woman I love."

"Long live the King!" shouted the London politicians and propagandists when the old King had abdicated and the new one was approaching the throne. And the people of London, the peers and the proletariat, all joined in and shouted: "Long live the King!" For loyalty is the badge of all their tribe.

What happened to the drunken slum-dweller who shouted facetiously in one of the pubs: "Long live the Duke!"—it is better not to record.

III

MORE FOG

London is a place. It is a place full of fog, where bright ideas are always welcome, provided they come in under quota and fill out the proper forms.

London has never failed to extend its hospitality to important thinkers who hold transcendental theories in any of the major intellectual fields. The entrance requirements are a change of clothes, a change of accent, and a change of appetite.

Freedom of speech, in London, is amply bestowed on everyone, even the most slovenly. In London's Hyde Park, a Communist is free to throw over the whole social order, provided he does not throw over any of the benches. In London's Piccadilly Circus, any atheist may freely blaspheme provided he joins in the chorus of "God Save the King!"

There is, in London, in the lowest as well as the highest circles, one mysteriously profane word. It is the forbidden *bloody*. London, in its present fog, does not remember why this word was originally forbidden. It once stood in abbreviation for "By Our Lady," before London began to forget.

London's social life is a ritual of accepted codes of conduct, and tempered tones of voice; accurate amounts of whiskey and proper proportions of soda. Any gifted alien who is willing to submit to these restrictions, or, at least, admit their reasonableness, is welcome to air there the fruits of his genius. George Bernard Shaw, an apostate Irish Catholic, was one who took advantage of this privilege. And so did Max Beerbohm, an apostate Mediterranean Jew. And, likewise, T. S. Eliot, an apostate Harvard Puritan.

London is a place. It is a spot. It is a point. It is a point at which England may be studied geometrically, even geographically, and, perhaps, genealogically. But it is never a point at which the native genius of the English may be suitably observed. "How many angels on the point of a pin?" was a frequent question in medieval Paris. "How many Angles on the point of an opinion?" is the constant problem in modern London.

London is a place—but not a good place in which to study Englishmen. The English character in London is involved in too many Empire employments, which kill off its spontaneity. The quintessential English traits are best seen out of London, in the country, as the English poets always knew, and as the English novelists eventually discovered.

Possibly these English traits may also be clearly seen by contrasting them with what is generally known of the traits of their perpetual neighbors and ancient foes, the Irish.

Psychologically considered—or should I say, nervously?—the world divides itself into two groups, the sentimental and the emotional. The English are sentimental. The Irish are emotional. And that is a clue to their differences and antipathies more valuable than any you will discover by examining the skulls of their prehistoric ancestors.

Emotion, which is the Irish expression of feeling, explodes and dissipates in short order. Sentiment, which is the English expression of the same, simmers and lingers on. The Irish "adore you" in brief splurges. The English "are fond of you" over protracted intervals. The volume of love received is ultimately about the same in either case. The Irish pour it on with a pitcher. The English sprinkle it through a fine hose.

The Irish are intense, positive, assertive, with an infinite capacity for hatred. The English are restrained, reticent, evasive, with an infinite capacity for contempt. The Irish have a hatred for the English contempt, just as the English have a contempt for the Irish hatred. Each nation thinks its to be the virtue, and the other's the vice. The Irish are, or imagine they are, a people of great pride. The English are, or fancy they are, a people of great modesty. But we shall see more about that as we go on.

The Irish make splendid soldiers; the English make splendid soldiers; the former by having inferior foes, the latter by having superior officers. An Irishman feels most like a soldier when he is shooting at an enemy. An Englishman feels most like a soldier when he is obeying a command. The Irish go forth to "die for their country" in a brief battle. The English enlist to "serve their country" for the duration of the war. The English usually win their wars, with the assistance of other nations. The Irish usually lose theirs, with the assistance of no one. The Irish "knocked the stuffings" out of the Black and Tans, and yet could not shake themselves free of England. The English managed "to relieve Mafeking" and thereby put an end to the uprising of the Boers. The English accuse the Irish of making continual fools of themselves in repeated rebellions known as "The Irish Cause." The Irish accuse the English of making perpetual fools of themselves in a sustained siege known as "The British Empire."

The Irish are a race of realists fighting for an ideal Ireland. The English are a race of idealists fighting for the England of the moment. The Irish want their country compact and undivided in one

small island. The English want theirs multiplied
and spread over the whole earth. The Irish want
Ireland to be little—but that is modesty! The English
want England to be large—but that is pride! And a
few paragraphs ago, weren't we putting it the other
way?

When an Englishman leaves England he refers to
it as "going abroad." When an Irishman leaves Ireland he refers to it as "leaving home." The Irish
have no king, but could use one. The English have a
king, but cannot find much for him to do.

The Irish defy anyone else to be Irish, and yet are
capable, in a particular case, of completely adopt-
ing as their own a full or partial stranger. The English insist that everyone else must be English, and
yet are always annoyed with the household acquired
by these forced naturalizations. DeValera is never
a Spaniard to the Irish. But Lloyd George is always
a Welshman to the English.

The Irish are born dogmatists; they want things
proved, and are thoroughly intolerant. The English
are born diplomats; they want things discussed, and
are thoroughly inconsistent. The Irish like their
whiskey straight, get drunk, and then take the pledge
for life. The English like their whiskey diffused in
soda water, overindulge, and then make a New
Year's resolution. An Englishman looks most intoxi-
cated before he has had anything to drink. An Irish-

man looks most sober when he has passed out of the picture.

The English, for centuries a ruling class, produce their best specimens in the form of servants—the English butler. The Irish, for centuries a servant class, produce their best specimens in the form of masters—the Irish squire. The English make splendid servants because they attach a sentiment to the function. The Irish make miserable servants because they attach none. The only time an Englishman ceases to be a good servant is when he becomes intimate with the family. The only time an Irishman ceases to be a bad servant is when he follows the same procedure.

If you want the English oozing out their sentiment in art, I offer James Hilton's *Good-bye, Mr. Chips,* the story of a pedantic little sissy, gurgling with gulps, whom every Irishman must find thoroughly insipid. If you want the Irish fuming forth their emotion in art, I offer Liam O'Flaherty's *The Informer,* the story of a raw-boned ruffian, blustering with oaths, whom every Englishman must find thoroughly revolting.

The Irish have a trick which drives me mad. It is their habit of saying a serious thing in a humorous way, and a humorous thing in a serious way. The English have a trick which exasperates me. It is their habit of saying an equally humorous or equally

43

serious thing with exactly the same expression of face and tone of voice.

How these two races, the English and the Irish, ever managed to sprout on adjacent islands, for the life of me, I cannot understand. The event may be taken as history's most flagrant example of a practical joke. Taken as groups, the English and the Irish are one hundred per cent incompatible. Yet, taken as individuals—so strange are the complementary requisites for romance—they can and do fall in love. Robert Emmet protested boldly that there never was a happy English-Irish political alliance. The late Cardinal Bourne declared he had never known of an unhappy English-Irish marriage. It was such a marriage that gave Robert Emmet to Ireland, and such a marriage that gave Cardinal Bourne to England.

But that will be enough about the British Isles. We must concentrate once more on London and London alone, for that is the theme of our study. And we must see if we cannot make the sun shine there, in some fashion, through some cloud, in some way, so as to illuminate the purpose, in God's scheme of things, of this great and important city.

London's highest altitude in religious aspiration is what is known as The Anglican Church. The term "Anglican" has come to denote the doctrinal content of this church. Its corporate title is "The

Church of England." Yet even in this, the most exalted of London's religions, there are various levels of belief. The Church of England is a welter of Low Church duties, Broad Church doubts, and High Church devotions. The head of The Church of England is not too familiar with its tenets, and not at all familiar with its ceremonies. He is the King of England, whom the Bishops (the *Episcopi*) have relieved of all sanctuary duties, synod attendance, and theological study. It is for this reason that The Church of England is sometimes referred to as "The Episcopal Church." Its monarch and its hierarchy avoid each other for the most part, and need dovetail in London only on elaborate occasions such as the dedication of a building, the betrothal of a duchess, or the burial of a queen.

I have said that London gives nothing racial or religious to any of its dependent territories. I should have added—except bad example. London's racial depreciations I have already censured. Its religious disedifications I should now like to expose.

London's religious roving is always in the form of some unholy unity revealing or concealing some unblessed trinity. London sustains a constant disdain for the Papal pattern of Church government established by Christ. London's parodies of this pattern are perverse: its divisions of sheep into many folds and its hirings of many shepherds.

"Thou art Peter, and upon this rock . . ." is Our

45

Holy Father the Pope, whom London divorced and dismissed. In his place are the substitutes established under the aegis of London's prestige: the bishops ("and upon these stones") of the Episcopal Church of the midlands of England; the ministers ("and upon these pebbles") of the Presbyterian Church of the highlands of Scotland; the pew-holders ("and upon these sands") of the Methodist Church of the lowlands of Wales. It was not enough for London's Anglican Church to be sectional within itself; it wanted to cause sections elsewhere. It was even eventually willing (one section of it) to become a section of the One and Holy Catholic Church, provided it could be incorporated into apostolic partnership with United Romans and Schismatic Greeks.

The Puritans fled from this London complexity and they pilgrimaged in search of a rock of their own. They found one in 1620, at Plymouth, and there they abandoned their boat. They later went north as far as Salem and Lynn, and then to Boston, where eventually they abandoned their beliefs. As complaining Calvinists they were excluded from England. In New England they developed into quiet Unitarians. Two memorials remain in Mayflower Boston of their former Puritan creed: a picturesque chapel named Trinity Church, and a railroad stop called Trinity Place.

Is Unitarianism the fruit of previous London influence? I shall give the answer in the form of a questionnaire. And I shall inflict it on a modern Bostonian, and in the best Unitarian manner.

Q. What is a Unitarian?

A. A Unitarian is one who believes in the unity of God and the trinity of enterprise.

Q. Can you give examples?

A. Shreve Crump and Low. Jones McDuffee and Stratton. Choate Hall and Stewart. New York New Haven and Hartford.

Q. *Who* and *what* are these?

A. Three prices in one pearl. Three stewards in one master. Three clients in one lawyer. Three journeys in one direction.

Q. What else are they?

A. An inevitable and rhythmic arrangement of names so proper as to make even commas between them superfluous. . . .

Q. In?

A. Decoration Utensilization Litigation Transportation. . . .

Q. Entitled?

A. Shreve Crump and Low. Jones McDuffee and Stratton. Choate Hall and Stewart. New York New Haven and Hartford.

Q. Are all these, Unitarians?

A. Unitarianism is not a synthesis.

Q. What is it?

A. An interpretation.

Q. Weren't its ancestors farmers, fishermen, and hunters?

A. Seed Weed and Feed. Hook Line and Sinker. Lock Stock and Barrel.

Q. In Boston, today, incorporated—what would they be called?

A. Farmsworth Fish and Huntington.

Q. You mentioned Jones McDuffee and Stratton.

A. Yes.

Q. It is hard to remember what they sell.

A. Plates Cups and Saucers.

Q. And the Shreve people are jewelers. . . .

A. And the Choate crowd are lawyers. . . .

Q. And the rest is a railroad.

A. Exactly.

Q. The Gospel doesn't make things quite so elemental.

A. Nothing is more elemental than sentimentality.

Q. But why such a blasphemous rejection of the beautiful processions in the Godhead? And why such a passion for partnerships that will blow to blazes on the Day of Doom?

A. These are extremely difficult questions to answer.

Q. Is Unitarianism a Revelation of its own? Is it an Illumination twirling all by itself in mid-ocean, like a solitary lighthouse, showing nothing, but itself, where to come, or go? Is it its own efficacious Grace?

48

A. These are extremely difficult questions to answer.

Q. Partnership is the weirdness of Anglicanism: High Broad and Low. Partnership is trying to sunder Catholicism: one root in three trees called The Branch Theory. Partnership is the horror of recent pray-as-you-enter projects: Dispersion Immersion and Conversion.

A. That is why a Unitarian prefers to remain. . . .

Q. What?

A. Transcendental.

Q. Like Emerson?

A. Like Shreve Crump and Low. Jones McDuffee and Stratton. Choate Hall and Stewart. New York New Haven and Hartford.

Q. You mean: minding his own kind of God?

A. Yes, and finding and founding his own kind of business.

This dialogue (now finished) with a Boston Unitarian may serve as an introduction to a London Jew. A Boston Unitarian and a London Jew have this in common: at neither end of the voyage does one discover a Christian; only pleasant remembrances of a household rejected; only happy acquaintances with a household refused.

The London Jew is, in points, identical with the Jew from all great capital cities. But comparisons

of him come clearest when he is contrasted with the
Jew from Berlin. The Jew from London is an idealist. The Jew from Berlin is an ideologist. The Berlin Jew has hopes for his thoughts. The London Jew
has hopes for his investments. Neither is the original
Jew from Jerusalem. And their defections can be
put most neatly in a deliberate play on words. The
one has stopped studying the Law and the Prophets.
The other has started studying the Profit and the
Loss.

One may ask who is responsible for what is known
as the London Jew—is it London, or is it the Jew? I
say it is London. I admit that London's Jew is responsible for his own unrest—as a despiser of the Old
and New Testaments for the sake of his old and
new investments. But the Bank of England was not
the escape the Rothschilds were looking for. It was
the escape that London's Calvinism provided. For
though London's liturgies are supported by Anglicanism, its morals are foundationed in Calvinism.
And Calvinism is the Christian support of usury.

Lutheranism is the Christian support of totalitar-
ianism; which is the obsession of the Jew from Berlin. When the Jew from the Holy Land went to the
Rhineland, he found Christian corruptions there
to ease his conscience and soothe his religious nostalgias. He found the Christian mind overplaying
itself at the expense of Christian values. He found
Luther's super-theology—his "Faith without good

works"—his belief in belief—his fatheadedness without performance—his frenzy without finesse. This gave the Jew from Jerusalem his chance to be a mental Messiah, and to start a procession of prophetic intellectualism that has lasted down to our day; and has included: Kant the super-philosopher; Hegel the super-ontologist; Heine the super-poet; Wagner the super-musician; Nietzsche the super-sociologist; Marx the super-economist; Freud the super-psychologist; Mann the super-Romanticist; Einstein the super-mathematician. All these Jewish versions of the Lutheran lead have contributed to the development of German intellectualism, and the collapse of German intelligence. The climax came when an apostate Catholic from Austria ran into Germany with a queer mustache, took over the militia, and out-Jewed the Jews. He became the super-German. And that was the end of Germany.

None of London's original thinkers can take rank with the German ideologists. London has a horror of abstract thought. London's philosophers are seekers of quick conclusions that will rationalize some form of London behavior. London turns out an original philosopher at the rate of about one a century. Its Seventeenth Century contribution was John Locke.

John Locke (1632-1704) was an experientialist. He believed that the proof of the pudding was in

51

the repeating. This London empiricism caused a criteriological revolt in nearby districts. George Berkeley (1684-1753) an Irish conceptualist, maintained that the eating of the pudding was in the proof. David Hume (1711-1776) a Scotch phenomenalist, held that the proof of the eating was in the pudding. And that accounts for all the philosophic thought that occurred in the British Isles for two centuries.

In London's out-of-town universities (Oxford to the north-left, and Cambridge to the north-right) abstract thought has always been treated with playful depreciation. Lectures are given with stately solemnity. But everything said before and after is a pleasant belittling of what has preceded or will follow. I once heard a Professor Durward from Cambridge lecture to the Oxford philosophical faculty on the subject, "Is Existence a Reality?" He decided during the lecture that it was not, and that all we could ever be sure of was this: at times there seems to be something, and at times it seems to be plural. But the lecture was only a prelude to a long evening of coffee drinking, during which time Professor Durward nearly exhausted himself trying pleasantly to assure us that he really was what he seemed to be, and that there was not, at the moment, more than one of him.

I once listened to some Oxford students discussing

the theory of metempsychosis (the transmigration of souls) after having come from a lecture in favor of it by a noted Oxford don. These students, instead of being outraged, or at least saddened, at an immortality offered to them in such degenerate form, were speculating with pleasure as to the especial brute each would like to become after death. One young man had antelope aspirations. Another could not bear not being a bear. It can be seen from this unwarranted whimsicality just what is meant by a London idealist. He is one to whom it does not matter what any idea stands for, as long as he can concrete it in some small London terms. He is one who is willing to take anything tangible in London and make it a matter of meditation for the rest of the world.

After the swift blight of London's crocus philosophers, the stage was set for England's most fantastic century in the realm of thought—the Nineteenth. This was the century which produced in academic circles two subjects never before heard of—economics and evolution. Economics is the history of the future. Evolution is the prophecy of the past.

Economics got its start north of London in some stingy thinking done by a Scotchman named Adam Smith, who had been banished in kilts from the Garden of Edinburgh. Economics moved into dignified discussion when a Protestant nobleman began plotting more revenue for the rich, and a Protestant minister began planning less progeny for the poor. These names were, respectively, the Honorable John Stuart Mill, and the Reverend Thomas Robert Malthus. What London's evolution twins, Darwin and Huxley, contributed to the cultural thought of the Nineteenth Century was the destruction of remembrances of the origin of sin, and the construction of resemblances in the origin of species.

Once London had persuaded itself that truth was unchaste, its restless religionists and romanticists were invited to roam in the areas of disreputable thought, in the hopes of securing beliefs by way of blandishments, in the hopes of securing certitudes by way of seductions. The Romantic Movement followed; so did the Oxford Movement; and after that, almost every petulant mental mood possible to man.

London's poets in the Nineteenth Century were not the best thinkers London had, but they were the most notable and quotable. Not one of London's poets in the whole Nineteenth Century was a true poet—not one. Each was a theorist selfishly exploring a doubt; not an artist gracefully affirming a certitude.

There is a way of making a study of London's Nineteenth Century poets. It is an unfair way, I admit, but it gets surprising results. It is to assume that every one of them is crazy.

Listen to Wordsworth:

If I should be where I no more can hear
Thy voice, nor catch from thy wild eyes these gleams
Of past existence. . . .

Or,

> The Child is Father to the Man. . . .

Here is Coleridge:

A damsel with a dulcimer
  In vision once I saw:
It was an Abyssinian maid,
  And on her dulcimer she played,
Singing of Mount Abora.
  Could I revive within me
Her symphony and song,
  To such a deep delight 'twould win me,
That with music loud and long,
  I would build that dome in air
That sunny dome! those caves of ice!
  And all who heard should see them there,
And all should cry, Beware! Beware!
  His flashing eyes, his floating hair!
Weave a circle round him thrice,
  And close your eyes with holy dread,
For he on honey-dew hath fed,
  And drunk the milk of Paradise.

And this is Robert Browning, gone stark mad:

55

> Gr-r-r—there go, my heart's abhorrence!
>> Water your damned flower pots, do!
> If hate killed men, Brother Lawrence,
>> God's blood, would not mine kill you!

and,

>> Like the skipping of rabbits by moonlight—
>>> three slim shapes
>> And a face that looked up . . . zooks, sir,
>>> flesh and blood,
>> That's all I'm made of. . . .

These London poets were not truly out of their minds. But they were truly out of their territories. They were looking for the secrets of eternal happiness in places where God had made no covenants, in the regions of aesthetic pleasure. And overstimulation by drink and overdepression by drugs are not the best moods for artistic creation. But most of London's poets failed to realize this for the whole of the Nineteenth Century.

When the Victorian era began in London, shyness and coyness became the required manners in wedded women and courtable girls. Humility and modesty were no longer admired. Men made big bows to delighted dames for the sake of graceful exercise, and paid large compliments to flattered females for the flow of rhetoric it caused. Rhetoric was most of what a lady listened to; poetry was most of what she was permitted to read. She read Wordsworth's "Intima-

tions of Immortality," a pre-natalist's belittling of
her at birth. She read Shelley's "Ode to the West
Wind," a pantheist's dismissal of her in destiny. She
read Keats' "Ode to Autumn," a serenade to the
sound of cider lingeringly oozing from a jug, a sen-
sualist's appraisal of her powers of appreciation.
For if

> "Beauty is truth, truth beauty,"—that is all
> Ye know on earth, and all ye need to know

and if a Georgian jug and a Grecian urn will alter-
nately and adequately serve its purposes, it is no wonder that this Keatsian recipe for rapture had many
a beautiful Victorian woman confused, and that she
turned for solace to other pursuits than the polite
perusal of poetry.

The Victorian woman was allowed to write a little
poetry herself, provided she had a brother (Dante
Gabriel Rossetti) or a husband (Robert Browning)
who could write it better than she could. If she did
not have a gifted man to sponsor her, she had to go
anonymous and assume a man's name. She had to
become Acton Bell, Currer Bell, and Ellis Bell,
whom nobody suspected for a long time were the
Brontë sisters—Ann, Charlotte and Emily. She had
to become George, for a change—George Eliot or
George Sand. An aunt and a niece (Katherine Har-
ris Bradley and Edith Emma Cooper) went unfem-

57

inine in unison, and called themselves Michael Field.

But perhaps the saddest of all the suppressed women in London's Nineteenth Century was little Emily Tennyson, who never wrote for publication, but followed her husband all around the house with a notebook and took down as apocalyptic everything he had to say. Alfred, Lord Tennyson, became famous for his Arthurian legends, in which he voyaged in verse in search of the Holy Grail (the cup that held the Precious Blood of Jesus) in the hopes of finding it empty. Emily Tennyson's notebooks were discovered after her death, and were found to be full of nothing worth remembering.

I have said before that more than one poet tried to escape from London, from its mental slavery and environmental fog. Some of the tragic escapes I have mentioned. A picturesque escape was that of bibulous John Masefield, who, after having dealt immoral London some metrical blows it will never forget, ran off to the United States and became a bartender in New York City. Here is what he wrote before he boarded the boat, in a poem called "London Town," of which I shall give three telling stanzas:

Oh, London Town's a fine town, and London sights
    are rare,
And London ale is right ale, and brisk's the London
    air,

And busily goes the world there, but crafty grows
    the mind,
And London Town of all towns I'm glad to leave
    behind . . .

Oh, London girls are brave girls, in silk and cloth
    o'gold,
And London shops are rare shops where gallant
    things are sold,
And bonnily clinks the gold there, but drowsily
    blinks the eye,
And London Town of all towns I'm glad to hurry
    by . . .

Oh, London tunes are new tunes, and London books
    are wise,
And London plays are rare plays, and fine to country
    eyes,
But wretchedly fare the most there and merrily fare
    the few,
And London Town of all towns I'm glad to hurry
    through . . .

London diplomats voted to recall this dangerous
Masefield, and made him poet laureate of England,
so that his earlier (his bartender) verse which was
all in reproof of London, might be overembroidered
with some official laudatory verse from a gifted
Masefield drinking in more quiet places. But Masefield, as London's official poet, has written nothing,
since he left the ranks of those who fare wretchedly
in Soho for those who fare merrily in Mayfair.

In any piece of poetry, when its origins are being studied, we may consider three things: the poet himself, the theme of his poem, and the art with which he expressed himself poetically. And we may call these three: the singer, the song, and the singing. And one is tempted, when the singing is agreeably good, to have pity on a poet whose self and whose song are not. And I think this pity is shared at times by God. For, out of the ranks of London poets, more than out of any other London group, have come conversions to the Catholic Faith in the last one hundred years.

Oscar Wilde was a London poet who died in the bosom of the Catholic Church. He did so after a life of riotous perversion and sin. He breathed his last in exile. It was in Paris, in a lonely garret, in direst poverty. Some Paris friend, full of French pity, brought him champagne to drink just before he died. As he feebly sipped and relished it, he made one last Wildean witticism. He said, "I am dying beyond my means." Applied to the undeserved gift in his hand, this final remark could have one significance; applied to the undeserved gift in his soul, it could have even a deeper one.

Among these eleventh hour conversions to the Catholic Faith, were two brilliant poets, who died in their early thirties—Lionel Johnson and Ernest Dowson. Both became Catholics after their popularity as writers was established, and had almost begun to wane.

Lionel Johnson was educated at Winchester, and at Oxford. His family for generations had been producing military men for London. But London, with its cheerful disillusionment and its impenitent lust, produced no inspiration for him. And, as poet, he tells it so in some burning stanzas addressed to it as to a dark angel. "Because of thee," he says, "no thought, no thing, abides for me undesecrate." And, he adds:

> Through thee, the gracious Muses turn
> To Furies, O mine Enemy!
> And all the things of beauty burn
> With flames of evil ecstasy.
>
> Because of thee, the land of dreams
> Becomes a gathering place of fears:
> Until tormented slumber seems
> One vehemence of useless tears.

It was no wonder that this lonely Londoner, who first began to be fond of the Irish, and then fond of their Faith, later found in both the purity of heart for which he was seeking.

Ernest Dowson was a London poet who entered the Catholic Church just in time to appreciate the beauty of its Last Sacraments. This weak-willed genius who had only this to say to his first love:

I have been faithful to thee, Cynara! in my fashion
and all of this to say to his false love:

> Life is a masque that changes.
> A fig for constancy!
> No love at all were better,
> Than love which is not free

found strength, by God's grace, to say to his last love,
this:

> Yet, when the walls of flesh grow weak,
> In such an hour, it well may be,
> Through mist and darkness, light will break,
> And each anointed sense will see.

And so did the soul of Ernest Dowson soar through
the mists of London's fog into the clear sky of re-
demption for which it was created.

I have never been able to make much sense out
of Dowson's short play *The Pierrot of the Minute*.
But I do know that the artist-poet who illustrated
it, Aubrey Beardsley, who came into the Catholic
Faith along with Ernest Dowson, died when he was
only twenty-six, just in time to profit by the Sacrament of Extreme Unction to which Dowson had paid
such loving tribute. And that was worth being a
smart boy for, in any one of the arts.

I think it can be seen from this brief summary of
the convert Catholic poets of London—who were

many more than the three I mention—that my heart is all in sympathy with them. I do not excuse their moral aberrations; but it was something to have repented of these in terms of the strict amendment of life required by the Catholic Church before one can enter it. Oscar Wilde, Lionel Johnson and Ernest Dowson, were *not* the three musicians referred to by young Beardsley when he wrote:

Along the path that skirts the wood,
The three musicians wend their way,
Pleased with their thoughts, each other's mood . . .
The morning's work, a new found theme, their
    breakfast, and the summer day.

But Baptism could be called "the morning's work"; and Faith "a new-found theme"; the Eucharist "their breakfast"; and Grace "the summer day" of Oscar Wilde, Lionel Johnson and Ernest Dowson, by way of their being Aubrey Beardsley's "The Three Musicians."

· The London Catholic poets who have ruined what chance the Catholic Faith might have had in England by way of aesthetic overture, were not the converted sinners who repented of their previous Protestant poetry. They were those who were either born in the Faith, or converted to it before they began to write their best work. They were such poets as Francis Thompson, Coventry Patmore, Alice Meynell and Gerard Manley Hopkins. These supposedly full-fledged Catholics sang songs which have been given to the world as specimens of what true Catholic poetry should be. But such is not the case.

The collected poems of Francis Thompson are like a shoe factory full of stained-glass windows. I know of no poet in whose work are combined so unpleasantly the machinery of verse and the embellishment of utterance. Here is a fair example:

Once—in that nightmare-time which still doth haunt
My dreams, a grim, unbidden visitant—
    Forlorn, and faint, and stark,
I had endured through watches of the dark
  The abashless inquisition of each star,
Yea, was the outcast mark
    Of all those heavenly passers' scrutiny;
    Stood bound and helplessly
For Time to shoot his barbed minutes at me;
Suffered the trampling hoof of every hour
    In night's slow-wheeled car;
  Until the tardy dawn dragged me at length
  From under those dread wheels; and, bled of
    strength,
    I waited the inevitable last.

Thompson writes a poem like a Turk weaves a rug. Even when he has only something trifling to say, it has to be plotted, schemed and indented like this:

    I saw thee only once,
    Although thy gentle tones

Said soft:
'Come hither oft.'

How any Catholic poet, after Our Lord's invitations—"Ask and you shall receive; seek and you shall find; knock and it shall be opened to you"—could conceive of eternal salvation as man, in the form of some ubiquitous fox, being chased by God in the form of a frothing "Hound of Heaven," is more than my generosities towards metaphors can find excuse for.

Francis Thompson's devastation of all other women, and his depreciation of the Mother of God, is his tribute to Alice Meynell.

Whose body other ladies well might bear
As soul,—yea, which it profanation were
For all but you to take a fleshly woof,
    Being spirit truest proof;
Whose spirit was lineal to that
    Which sang *Magnificat*.

Of London's Alice Meynell it is difficult to speak. She came into the Catholic Church, and called herself a Catholic. But what she believed in, I do not know. Perhaps the salvation of the solar system, for Christianity seems to have meant to her a series of celestial incarnations. She wrote:

                . . . in the Eternities
Doubtless we shall compare together, hear

65

A million alien Gospels, in what guise
He trod the Pleiades, the Lyre, the Bear.

Alice Meynell had a superabundance of Christian
affection for stars of any kind, particularly artists
and poets. Her list of Babylon admirers included
John Ruskin, George Meredith, Robert Browning,
E. V. Lucas, Matthew Arnold, Algernon Charles
Swinburne, W. E. Gladstone, Neville Lytton and
John Singer Sargent. Her Jerusalem associates were,
of course, Coventry Patmore, Francis Thompson
and Wilfrid Meynell.

What virtue allowed her to do never interested
Alice Meynell. Her fascination was what virtue
forced her to forego. Here is the graceful expression of her tyranny over herself:

I must not think of thee; and, tired yet strong,
   I shun the thought that lurks in all delight—
   The thought of thee—and in the blue Heaven's
      height,
And in the sweetest passage of a song.
Oh, just beyond the fairest thoughts that throng
   This breast, the thought of thee waits hidden yet
      bright;
   But I must never, never come in sight;
I must stop short of thee the whole day long.

But when sleep comes to close each difficult day,
   When night gives pause to the long watch I keep
   And all my bonds I needs must loose apart,
Must doff my will as raiment laid away,

66

With the first dream that comes with the first sleep
I run, I run, I am gathered to thy heart.

G. K. Chesterton, after she had said, "Were I a
man, I had been Chesterton," called Alice Meynell
"a message from the sun."
I think that Alice Meynell was, rather, a fascinating bird, whose shadow here and there, on far too
many windowpanes, obscured, at intervals, the message from the Son of God.

Coventry Patmore was a London poet who, while
laboring in the British Museum, became enamored
of the illustrative possibilities of love. Here is one of
his early epigrams:

> He does not rightly love himself
> Who does not love another more.

Patmore's first declarations concerning love were
put in a set of poems called *The Angel in the House.*
In this book what is secret about married love he revealed. After his conversion to the Catholic Faith,
he wrote a book about God, called *The Unknown
Eros,* in which what is revealed about Divine Love
he endeavored to conceal.
Coventry Patmore married, successively, three
times. He was blissfully happy in each betrothal,
tenderly tearful at each bereavement. He was continually going from a wedding to a wake, from a
candle to a cake. Each of his wives was let know in

verse that his love for her was not his love of God. She was also metrically informed that his love for God would not interfere with his love for her, not even if she were in Heaven, and he in Hell.

After his conversion to the Catholic Faith, Coventry Patmore came to know a maiden too singular for any of his theories. She was the Blessed Virgin Mary, the Mother of God.

Patmore began with a distaste for the way Our Lady is loved by simple Catholics. He was chilled and revolted at what seemed to him the excess of many forms of devotion to her. He could not abide the Rosary. He endeavored to correct this defect by submitting to the mind of the Church, and by disciplining himself with a pilgrimage to Lourdes.

After his visit to Lourdes, Coventry Patmore felt equal to the task of writing poems in praise of Our Lady. He wrote many of these. They are full of skillful metaphors and exuberant phrases. But even after the most astute studies of her value, he found her not too singular, not even in her virginity. All virgins, he believed, experienced in their own way what Our Lady experienced in hers.

In a poem addressed to her as *Regina Coeli,* he wrote:

> True Virgin lives not but does know
> (Howbeit none ever yet confess'd)
> That God lies really in her breast,
> Of thine He made His special nest!

Simple Catholic devotion makes the presence of God in a virgin's breast no Incarnation. It calls the Incarnation the presence of the God-Man in a Virgin's womb. There was only one such Virgin-Mother.

In another of Patmore's Marian poems the pragmatic value of Our Lady is appraised. He calls her:

Our only Saviour from an abstract Christ.

I do not want to dismiss harshly any poet who has spoken, even vaguely or in vanity, concerning the Mother of God. And so I shall say that after a long life of erotic anguish which did not, because of its quality, truly include the Blessed Virgin Mary,

One day in autumn when foliage was falling
And colors were coming to a close,
When warmth was turning into winter
And skies were turning into snows

there was no more Patmore admitting into poetry the unfitting improprieties of prose.

Gerard Manley Hopkins was born at Stratford, a suburb of London. After his conversion to the Catholic Church and entrance into the Society of Jesus, he later served for a while as a Jesuit priest in London. His life was spent teaching outmoded subjects and writing poems no one was ready to read.

Gerard Manley Hopkins is, on his own admission, an odd poet. Everything in his technique is odd, even his rhymes, of which rhymes he remarks that they are the kind which "malignity may munch at, but the Muses love."

Modern critics are wont to refer to Father Hopkins as an obscure poet. It is my belief that he is odd, but not obscure.

The obscurity one finds in Father Hopkins is surface obscurity: curious arrangement of words, omissions and ellipses, use of outmoded verbs and nouns and, above all, a constant confusion of his reader's mind by a willful, almost wicked, employment of homophones. Father Hopkins' obscurity might well be called "jig-saw puzzle obscurity." But once you have the clue and know how to decipher him, even the most difficult lines come clear. This decoding of a poet's message is, may I add, not aesthetic pleasure. It is mere curiosity pleasure. And there are times when Father Hopkins gives his reader altogether too much of it.

Let me take as an example of Father's obscurity, what is reputedly one of his most obscure pieces. The poem to which I refer is called:

TOM'S GARLAND:
upon the Unemployed

and it runs as follows:

Tom—garlanded with squat and surly steel
Tom; then Tom's fallowbootfellow piles pick

70

By him and rips out rockfire homeforth—sturdy
    Dick;
Tom Heart-at-ease, Tom Navvy: he is all for his
    meal
Sure, 's bed now. Low be it: lustily he his low lot
    (feel
That ne'er need hunger, Tom; Tom seldom sick,
Seldomer heartsore; that treads through, prick-
    proof, thick
Thousands of thorns, thoughts) swings though.
    Commonweal
Little I reck ho! lacklevel in, if all had bread:
What! Country is honour enough in all us—lordly
    head,
With heaven's lights high hung round, or, mother-
    ground
That mammocks, mighty foot. But no way sped,
Nor mind nor mainstrength; gold go garlanded
With, perilous, O no; nor yet plod safe shod sound;
    Undenizened, beyond bound
Of earth's glory, earth's ease, all; no one, nowhere,
In wide the world's weal; rare gold, bold steel,
    bare
    In both; care, but share care—
This, by Despair, bred Hangdog dull; by Rage,
Manwolf, worse; and their packs infest the age.

This is tortured expression, if there ever was any.
It is neither prose nor poetry. It is not even English.
Let me take the poet's thought out of the uncom-
fortable jargon in which it is enmeshed, and see what

he is trying to say in straightforward language. Here is what "Tom's Garland" means. (The subtitle, may I add, is not a censure on those who are out of work, but on those who will not work, even when work is offered, by employing their talents, however simple and blunt they may be, for the common good.)

Tom the day laborer has a garland just the same as a king has.

Tom's garland is not a gold crown on his head, but steel nails in his boots (squat and surly steel).

When the day's work is done, both Tom, and that boob (that fallowbootfellow) who works alongside of him all day, throw down their picks and shovels, and as they walk home for supper, the nails in their boots make sparks on the stone pavement; in other words, they "rip out rockfire homeforth." Dick, Tom's fellow workman is, by the way, a brawny man (sturdy Dick).

Tom is carefree when his day's work is over, Tom the workman.

And he has a good appetite for supper.

And after supper he is practically ready to go to bed.

I grant you that Tom's lot is a low one; but he never needs to starve (food being his main concern), and he lives through his low lot with a gusto. One seldom finds him sick, and almost never depressed.

72

His mind is immune (prickproof) to worrisome
thoughts. No matter how many thousands of
thoughts try to worry him, as they would you or
me, Tom easily throws them off.

When it comes to giving all we have by way of
talent to the common good (Commonweal),
the fact that one man has few talents and another has many, is no true hardship, provided
everyone has enough to eat.

It is satisfaction enough for each one to know that
he can work for the common good; whether he
be a king, whose head is crowned with gold, and
whose brilliance is mental and heavenly, or
whether he be a big-footed yokel who tills the
earth and lives all with his muscles.

But those folk who will do nothing for the common good, neither through brains nor brawn,
what about them? Are they crowned like a king
with dangerous honors? No. Nor do they get the
comforts of the workingman with his big boots.

They have no home amongst us, and they get
neither earth's glory nor earth's ease. They are
practical nobodies, with no purpose serving
the common good. They have neither the king's
gold crown nor the navvy's steel-nailed boots.
And they get the worst out of both avocations.
They get bored as kings do, without being kings;
and they become full of rage and resentment

73

like the laborer on a strike (an even worse af-
fliction).
And there are plenty of these nobodies (these
unemployed) in our midst today.

The above is a hurried paraphrase of what the
poem means. We now see what is being said, but not
because the message was essentially obscure. The
poem is full of the most commonplace statement.
The devices of expression, however, are so helter-
skelter and queer, that the poem looks obscure when
one first reads it. By no authentic test can this hodge-
podge be called a poem. There are not two succes-
sive lines in it that one could—or would want to
—remember. There is nothing of the obscurity of
mystery in it; there is only the obscurity of problem.
And once the problem is solved, one wants nothing so
much as never to bother with the thing again.

No one can deny that there are in the poems of
Father Hopkins phrases of jewel-like beauty, indeed
diamonds. But poets are supposed to offer all jewels
—not unquarried fields of thought in which the
reader is invited to dig.

When Gerard Manley Hopkins died, no one in
the English Province of the Jesuit Order thought his
poems were truly Catholic or Ignatian. And so a
group of British Protestants were allowed to edit
and annotate his work. Robert Bridges was given his
poems; Humphry House presided over his diaries;

and Claude Colleer Abbott took charge of his letters.

Father Hopkins was born in 1844 and died in 1889. To indicate the extent of his dislocation during life, he wrote: "I always knew in my heart Walt Whitman's mind to be more like my own than any other man's living. And as he is a very great scoundrel, this is not a pleasant confession."

It is merely a pleasant lack of contrition and very little purpose of amendment.

London is a place. It is a place full of fog—as its poetic expressions, psychological confessions, and weather reports will agree.

IV

LONDON SPRING

A skyful of frustrated fertility known as pollen, floating northwestward from the gardens of Denmark and Holland, and hanging over the fields of England, is what constitutes a London fog. Supermillions of microspores—germs of flowers on their way to becoming seed—are suffused into the moistures of the British air. These form the nuclei of infinitesimally small clouds, which, in turn, cluster together, and envelop hill and horizon with a dismal drapery of gloom. It is hard to know what to call this unwelcome weather, but it has come to be identified by a monosyllable sounding like a horn mournfully blowing in the midst of it.

Fog—is the one subject London poets, while perpetually confronted with it, have kept away from.

76

But in those lovely months of the year, in late April, May and early June, when London's imported pollen is busy back in its own gardens on the Continent, the fog over London lifts; its skies are clear; the sun shines continually; and everyone rejoices, because it is Spring. And this is the one subject no London poet has ever been able to avoid.

Place and weather are powerful components in the making of human drama; and the Providence of God, which is nothing if not dramatic, lets a city's climate be a reminder, and sometimes a corrective, of its spiritual ills. London's fog and London's lack of faith go together. And were London to regain its faith, the Will of God might find a hundred meteorological and agricultural reasons for sending Danish and Dutch pollen elsewhere to form fog, and might let London's sunshine alone.

London lost the Faith by loving God without its soul. Paris lost the Faith by loving God without its strength. Berlin lost the Faith by loving God without its mind. And Rome lost the Faith by loving God without its heart. But a nation, to secure salvation, must—and especially in its central city—love God with its whole heart, its whole soul, its whole mind, and its whole strength. And it must love it that other nations do likewise.

Along with the Faith, London lost also its sense of eternal things—happiness and joy. It retained only their temporal and weak equivalents—a continual contentment known as pleasure, an intermittent excitement known as delight.

Pleasure has been London's favorite feminine feeling ever since the Sixteenth Century, just as delight has been its major masculine mood. "It will be a pleasure!" London ladies are required to say, when some extra kindness is expected of them. "I shall be delighted!" is the routine response of every over-willing London male when some perfunctory courtesy is called for.

Just as fog in London's sky is the symbol of its loss of Faith, two parodies of London's empty pleasure and false delight perpetually prowl in its dim-lit streets. They are London's stray cat, London's lost dog.

A cat is contentment. A dog is excitement. A cat is pleasure. A dog is delight. A cat is pleasure, contentedly purring and licking its paws. A dog is delight, excitedly barking and wagging its tail. A cat is all eyes in the darkness; a dog all ears in the stillness of London's interminable night.

Because London did not give up God through its mind, its strength, or its heart, persons still prevail there as the leading symbols of excellence. There is never any London movement to which can be applied some bombastic name like "Kulturkampf"; some ruthless title like "Nazism"; or some weak indication like "Action Française." Persons may be crowded together in London, and underpaid, and undernourished, and overharassed by hardship; but persons they still remain. Even political London produced, right in our own day, a character as singular as Winston Churchill.

I hold no brief for the sanctity of Winston Churchill. But the preciousness which God put in him by way of making him unique, he has been decent enough to preserve. Sociologists interested in specimens, and psychologists interested in types, never study Churchill. No one can possibly classify him. He is, as the sane old saying goes, "in a class by himself."

Here is an amusing story told of Churchill. During his term as Prime Minister of England, the Anglican Archbishop of Canterbury died. The appointment of a successor was being discussed. Churchill blurted out:

"Do you think Hinsley would take it?"

"Hinsley, sir!" cried all his Protestant cohorts, indignantly, and almost with a single voice, "is the Roman Catholic Archbishop over at Westminster Cathedral."

"Oh, that's right," said Churchill, cheerfully; letting the incident drop without a single syllable of apology.

Personality can never be defined. Realization of personality can come only by repeated willingness to acknowledge it. A relish for personality is the fruit of countless experiences, all of which, when added, constitute the unit with which one started. Awareness of personality is an art bestowed by God on anyone willing to accept it. This art the English have been willing to accept.

We now see the hidden secret of London's deep and abiding loyalty to things. It is the stubborn hold it has always managed to keep on the value of personality, even when its other certitudes began to fail. Every Londoner somehow speaks to you as though there were a hidden majesty in your nature, which he was endeavoring to discover. Let his motive be selfish, if you will; it is still preoccupied with a self. Likewise, every Londoner speaks from a hidden dignity of his own, which no amount of hardship can manage to take from him.

It is this urge for personality that keeps a London king on his throne when his rule has become useless; that makes even the very street and number where a Prime Minister of London dwells, an address to be written and spoken with respect; that lets colleges at London's universities go on being called "Christ Church," and "Jesus College," and "Magdalen," and "Trinity," when there is no longer any creed within their walls to support these once hallowed titles.

It is this unrelinquished relish for personality that preserves mystical meaning in outmoded London words. "Zounds!" means "By God's wounds."

"Bedlam" is a corruption of Bethlehem. And "hocus pocus" is a syllabic collapse of the sacred and personal words ("Hoc est enim Corpus Meum") which a Catholic priest speaks at the Consecration of the Mass.

Berlin never retained this hunger for person and personal prerogatives, which still haunts London. Berlin gave up its mind to the study of mentality. Germans are proud. Paris concentrated its strength on the exercise of the weakest of vices. Frenchmen are sensual. Rome alienated its heart to foreign lands for the sake of revenue, and of religious retinue. Italians are greedy. London did none of these things. London's soul went sour, and its desires went too far abroad for its own happiness at home. Englishmen are gluttons.

But the mind, the strength, and the heart of London have always stayed riveted in royal allegiance to a once sacrosanct value it knew—the preciousness of personality, bequeathed to it in the days when its land was Catholic, its Faith dogmatic, and its heroes well-named and well-remembered saints.

An instinct for personality is requisite for a response to the overtures of Christian Revelation. God's cry from the depths of Eternity is personal. It comes from three distinct Persons, Who are Divine. They are: the Father, the Son, and the Holy Ghost. This is the Everlasting Godhead.

The Second Person of this Most Blessed Trinity has, because of love, become the bridge between two impassibles, the infinite and the finite. He is the motherless Son of a Father in Eternity, and the fatherless Child of a Virgin in time.

Our Lord taught us that there can be no Revelation without apostles, and no sanctity without saints. This Christian concreteness in consecrated things London has never disliked. St. George, slaying the Dragon, is virtue triumphing over vice, to London's satisfaction. London's German cousins from the Continent, have endeavored to depreciate St. George of England. They claim to have scholarly statistics to show that he never existed. But London has no use for German hagiologists, nor for Belgian Bollandists. St. George will continue to slay the Dragon as long as London lasts.

French fussiness is also a trait that has never tainted the London temperament. *Liberté, égalité, fraternité,* as a call to action, would leave Londoners lying in their beds. London's late sleepers pay no attention to any summons which has not in it the noise of newsboys shouting in the streets.

London's strong sense of personality is closely allied to its sense of chivalry. London loves a woman it can call a queen. Failing of that, a duchess, a marchioness, or a countess will somehow do. And a princess will do perfectly.

At every point in English history where circumstances have caused a queen—by way of an interval between kings—to be in command of England, there have been courtesy, consideration, and compliments always waiting to greet her.

London would rather have a queen in fiction than a goddess in mythology. Even a London cat on the loose, and missing for a few nights from its own neighborhood, is regally interrogated upon her return:

> Pussy cat! Pussy cat!
> Where have you been?

To this she must answer:

> I've been to London
> To visit the Queen,

or no one will believe her.

The best recipe for royalty, according to The Second Book of Machabees, Chapter 7, Verse 21, is "the joining of a man's heart to a woman's thought." This is the formula for valiancy in a woman, and for chivalry in a man.

The Norman invasion of England added a French flourish to London's sense of chivalry. London did not mind the Norman conquest too much because it acquired from it such a bright and new vocabulary. After the coming of William the Conqueror, there were two languages fighting it out in London, impolite Anglo-Saxon, and terribly polite French. The

English language immediately adapted itself to this dualism. What was called pig in the pen was called pork on a platter. What in France was the form, was in England the matter. What was sheep in the fold, became mutton served cold. And a cow in the stable, was beef on the table.

Queen Anne, an English queen who spoke only French, and who ruled England affectionately for forty-nine years (1665-1714), had a fondness for little cakes, which she called, in her own language, "petits gateaux." "Petticoats" was the best the ears of London cooks could make out of "petits gateaux"; and so "Queen Anne's petticoats" have been London's favorite little cakes since the early part of the Eighteenth Century.

French courtesy was one thing to take from the Norman Conquest. Graeco-Roman culture was quite another. Greek is the culture of the mind. Latin is the culture of the heart. Greek is the illustration of truth. Latin is the symbolization of love. The two in providential, almost miraculous union, have constituted the Graeco-Roman culture, the greatest culture civilization has ever known. And it is important to remember that it was by way of a French channel of land, as well as by an English channel of water, that this culture flowed through France into England.

It is also well to remember that as Athens and

Rome passed through Paris, they became inextricably confused, one with the other. The Classics did not enter England in clear overture. It was always by way of French complication. A cultivated Frenchman is constantly surprising and disappointing you. He is cold where you thought he would be friendly, affectionate where you expected him to be aloof. He is either a Greek who lives in the Latin Quarter, or a Latin who falls asleep in the Parthenon.

Greece and Rome, issued into London by way of a French aqueduct, and the loving London heart, and the resolute London mind, had no power to cope with them according to the French formula. And so Athens and Rome divided again, once they reached London. All the heads went resolutely into the universities, and all the hearts went regretfully into the gutter.

Even among classically educated Englishmen— and there are many such—because they have no heart for the cultivation they have acquired, one is constantly hearing the expression: "I know a little Latin, and less Greek." And of perhaps no scholars in the world is this statement less generally true.

The British Foreign Policy is the result of most careful mental calculation, assisted by most resolute abandonment to fortune. An empire has been the fruit of this. It has not been the Graeco-Roman Empire. It has been the empire of a John Bull and a

Johnny-on-the-Spot—the one at a desk in nearby
Downing Street, the other on a deck in distant Dakar.

This Empire of Britain, so alertly London-con-
trolled, is unmistakably the empire of a queen. Indeed, there were probably no London rulers who
contributed more to its efficient well-being than the
London queens, notably Queen Victoria. All the slogans and mottoes phrased to encourage Britain's
Empire, such as "Britannia Rules the Waves," are
those which touch allegiance as to a queen. And
this took courage, for in the extension and further-
ance of London's Empire, the greatest obstacles it
ever encountered were the queen-hating nations of
the world, including India, the land of the culture
and the religion of misogyny, as it is practiced by
the pure oriental Hindu and the quasi-occidental
Mohammedan.

Of Mohammedanism, I know more than I do of
Hinduism; though of the two grouped together, I
know plenty. Mohammed allowed many wives and
no wine, by way of showing his liturgical esteem for
the respective value of each. The fruit of Mohammed's teaching in India has been the having, along
with many women, of as much wine as a Mohammedan cares to, provided he pretends there is a doc-
trine on the subject, and bows his head towards
Mecca.

"There is no God but Allah, and Mohammed is
the prophet of Allah!" is utterance in cold, reli-

gious frenzy, as far away from a London salute to God and queen as the dead deserts of mid-India are from the bright, rippling waters of the Thames.

If London is disliked precisely because of its world prestige, world politics, and world propaganda, then one is still confronted with the problem—if one believes in God—as to why God created it, and gave it such prominence, and populated it so abundantly. Is it that He made eight million mistakes, all in a restricted area?

I think the answer is clear. God does not approve of London. But God, Who loved India, when it was willing to take the message of His Child from Saint Francis Xavier, now despises it. India is, in our day, the most Mary-hating nation in the world. London will receive no eternal reward for muzzling the Moslem and hindering the Hindu. London's reward is entirely on this earth. But Mohammedan and Hindu damnation are, thank God, and thanks to London, both in eternity, and in time.

I cannot leave the horrid land of Mahatma Gandhi, that bed-sheeted little Hindu intellectual, without despairing at what he did to the soul of an Indian girl I once admired.

Sarojini Naidu, in the days when she visited London, read its literature and listened to its ladies talk. Whereupon, she concocted for the English an exquisite frailty in a poem. It is called "The Song of the Palanquin Bearers." A palanquin is a royal

stretcher, upon which a queen, or a bride, is carried
on the shoulders of men. Here is the soft, haunting
song Miss Naidu sang:

Lightly, oh lightly, we bear her along,
 She sways like a flower in the wind of our song;
She skims like a bird on the foam of a stream,
 She floats like the laugh from the lips of a dream.

Gaily, oh gaily, we glide and we sing;
 We bear her along like a pearl on a string.

Softly, oh softly, we bear her along,—
 She hangs like a star in the dew of our song.
She springs like a beam from the brow of a tide,
 She falls like the tear from the eye of a bride.

Gaily, oh gaily, we glide and we sing;
 We bear her along like a pearl on a string.

The British Empire is a collection of disunited
lands and nations, dominated by taking swift advantage of every dissension. The overt act by which
Henry VIII indicated to the world the pattern of
England's apostasy, was a divorce of his throne from
the Chair of Peter, and a divorce of himself from
his lawful Queen. With both its spiritual and its secular interests the fruit of unwedded allegiances, it is
no wonder there is no unity in what London does.
It has lost all sense of the unity of a bridegroom and
a bride.

88

Yet something still stays in England, which I do not know what to call. By way of showing how full of promise and emptiness it is, I call it "London Spring." It is spring without summer; promise without fulfillment; style without substance; manners without meaning.

Every English sailor salutes the quartermaster's deck when he passes it, aboard ship. On it there used to be a statue of the Blessed Virgin Mary. No sailor would pass it without acknowledging it. The Mary images have been removed from English ships. But the empty salutes still go on.

I once heard John Galsworthy lecture in the refectory of one of Oxford's colleges. He entered, dressed in clerical robe and hat, and stood at one end of the refectory, in the manner of a visiting abbot. He saluted an empty niche in the wall. This again was a place where a statue of the Blessed Virgin used to be kept, and is kept no longer.

The Oxford and Cambridge colors are blue. Oxford has dark blue. Cambridge light blue. This is in honor of the colors in Mary's mantle. God's Mother has departed. Nothing remains, but the color of her dress.

And so, on and on we could go, through all the English emptiness, through all the haunted places. A sweet odor lingers everywhere, but a death and a departure have most surely occurred. Maurice Bar-ing, just before he died, put on paper the sad summary of it all. It was his beautiful study of *The Lonely Lady of Dulwich*.

The Lonely Lady of Dulwich is the English girl, still trying to hold out to her husband and to her household, the dowry which was once hers, when she was the assured image of the Mother of God. Indoors has become too stuffy for her, so she has gone out for good into the garden. She is constantly tending flowers. The lily is her favorite; and, also, the rose.

Her coat-of-arms is a little English heart, with three French words written across it: "Saignant et brûlant," which means, "bleeding and burning." This is the heart of the London girl since the Lady of Walsingham went away.

V

CLOUDS OVER LONDON

We might begin with the parochial and plain sermons of John Henry Newman to justify the title of this chapter. Newman was a cloud over London. His parochial and plain sermons were his effort to become a clear day.

I call John Henry Newman a cloud to distinguish him from a fog. I believe he was a hindrance to the sunshine of London on the very days when the sun was shining. The sun in the sky can be likened, and not unfairly, to the light of Faith. This is what Holy Scripture calls it—the very Holy Scripture that explains to us how and why both sky and light were made. John Henry Newman was a delineated darkness in front of this sun. He was conspicuous only for the rays of sunlight that streamed around him.

John Henry Newman was in mind and in strength a Catholic. He was in heart and in soul an Anglican. To John Henry Newman, the Catholic Faith did not come from hearing. It came from quiet reading. He assented to the Pope; he sympathized with Pusey.

John Henry Newman spent most of his life justifying the values of Faith as they occur in the cold intellectual territories of what he considered to be the cultured mind. He makes a most disparaging distinction between Faith and Devotion. To every simple Catholic—and certainly to every saint—Faith without Devotion is dead Faith—Faith without life, a *fides mortua*—as opposed to a *fides viva* of the Latin theologians. To John Henry Newman, Faith and Devotion are distinct both in fact and in idea. "We cannot," he says, "be devout without faith, but we may believe without feeling devotion." His overt devoirs are addressed to Faith; his subtle disparagements directed towards Devotion.

John Henry Newman was resolutely a Catholic. He was also apologetically and regretfully so. It was regret, which, of course, he did not regret. His mind and strength would not allow him to do so. But it was regret for which he was constantly apologizing —defending it when it was attacked, proposing it when anyone started to forget it.

After entering the Catholic Church, and being ordained to the Catholic priesthood, and being bounteously empowered to offer the Holy Sacrifice of the Mass each morning at a Catholic altar, John Henry Newman at evening could be expected to burst into tears at the remembrance of how beautiful Evensong sounded in the Vesper Service of the Anglican Church he had abandoned. One of his repeated utterances was that he was afraid he could never be a saint, because he loved the pagan classics so intensely.

John Henry Newman was constantly praised for the clarity of his English prose and the limpid lucidity of his style. That he possesses these qualities, no one can deny. But his is the cold clarity of clear water in a fish bowl, in which one looks in vain for the fish.

Newman achieved his clarity of style by a scorn for the following devices of expression: (a) the parable; (b) the proverb; (c) hyperbole; (d) litotes; (e) the syllogism; (f) the enthymeme; (g) the analogy; (h) the allegory; (i) aposiopesis; and (j) the periodic sentence. Most other writers have thought that human utterance at its best is full of divisions, distinctions, approaches, overstatements and understatements, strong and gentle comparisons, and a not-too-rigid adherence to etymology—so as to enable our almost-clear thoughts, ever mixed with

93

feeling and frailty, to be conveyed lovingly and in human fashion to our kind and expressed to our kindred. Not so John Henry Newman.

John Henry Newman is constantly talking to the perfect citizen of Plato's *Republic,* to an elected candidate for More's *Utopia*—to Adam in the Garden of Paradise just after he ate the apple, and just before he covered himself with leaves.

ˎ The more you read Newman, the less you remember what he says. He is an author whom it is impossible to quote. What you recall, after you have finished reading him, is never what the clarity of his style was revealing, but some small, unwarranted queerness that it was almost concealing. You remember that Newman said that a chandelier "depends" from a ceiling; and if you look up "depends" in the dictionary, you will find that "hangs from" is exactly what it means. You remember that Newman felt entitled to mispronounce deliberately one English word, to show his proprietorship over the language. He pronounced "soldier" as *sol—dee—err*. You remember that Newman was perpetually fussing about Reverend E. B. Pusey, who seems, in some refined way, to have gotten under his skin.

You remember Newman was shocked that Catholics were giving Protestants the grounds for declaring that "the honor of Our Lady is dearer to Catholics than the conversion of England," as though anything else could be the childlike truth. You

remember that Newman particularly disliked the
Marian writings of St. Alfonso Liguori, a Doctor of
the Universal Church, and said of these writings,
"They are suitable for Italy, but they are not suitable
for England." You remember that, with regard to
the Immaculate Conception of the Blessed Virgin
Mary, Newman insisted, in scholarly fashion, that
"her case is essentially the same as St. John the Bap-
tist, save for a difference of six months"—which is
precisely the difference this dogma demands. You
remember that though Newman was in favor of
Papal Infallibility, he was not in favor of its being
infallibly defined by the Pope.

And then, all of a sudden, you do not want to remember anything else you remember from Newman,
not even the clarity of his style.

I have said in the last chapter that London poets
had no certitudes; only theories, artistically phrased.
I shall make two exceptions to this statement. They
are the poets Thomas Hardy and A. E. Housman.
Both of these poets had certitudes—the certitudes
that go with despair. Their heyday was the very end
of the Nineteenth Century. In the Twentieth Century they faded, in realistic fulfillment of their own
disconsolate songs.

John Henry Newman always gave one the impression that he was—to use his own phrase—a
"kindly light amidst the encircling gloom." Hardy

and Housman ambitioned to be unkindly glooms in the midst of a light that had vanished.

Hardy was at one time an architect's apprentice in London. Housman, who was in early life a stupid boy in college, and at the end of his life a professor in a learned university, spent a good deal of his time in between these assignments being a clerk in a London patent office. There is, almost mystically, a melancholy architecture signatured in all of Hardy's poems; and Housman seems to have his own gloomy thoroughness in uttering despair, patented. His lines are inimitable, no matter how simple and sad they may look.

There never were two poets who, in their own lifetimes, were more recognized and more appreciated than Hardy and Housman. Both spent their middle and later years in comparative wealth, surrounded with adulation. Both wrote their poems, even the most plaintive of them, at the period of England's greatest material prosperity. It was long before our modern wars. It was a time when conviviality, good wages for all, and plenty of holidays were London's regular routine. Neither Hardy nor Housman seems to have been tragically disappointed in love. At least, no particular woman seems to have been especially mean to either, as women were reported to have been to the drunken and drugged poets of the same era. Both Hardy and Housman, particularly Housman, made pretense to be heavy drinkers; but it is quite clear they were not. They were reflective drinkers—ale sippers—flavoring their own despairs with mouthfuls of light alcohol.

How did these two, Hardy and Housman, ever manage, in the midst of so much temporal well-being, to touch moods of such classic and perfect despair? The answer is that Hardy and Housman were the poets laureate of a London that had lost its soul. It was theirs to have tasted anticipated damnation and literal hell on earth.

An early London saint, the Venerable Bede, gives five reasons why God lets man suffer sickness on this earth. (1) For an increase of merit, as in the case of Job. (2) For the preservation of humility, as in the case of St. Paul. (3) For the correction of sin, as in the case of Miriam, the sister of Moses. (4) For the glory of God, as in the case of the man born blind, whose miraculous cure is related in the ninth chapter of St. John. (5) For the beginning of damnation, as in the case of Herod, who slaughtered the Holy Innocents.

Housman and Hardy had a soul sickness that puts them clearly in Herod's class.

Housman often mentions God: (a) for the sake of emphasis:

> And naked to the hangman's noose
> The morning clocks will ring
> A neck God made for other use
> Than strangling in a string

(b) to win sympathy for an interesting proverb:

> And malt does more than Milton can
> To justify God's ways to man

or (c) to support his own anger or bewilderment:

> Oh, I have been to Ludlow Fair
> And left my necktie God knows where.

But the dead showdown of Housman's cold hatred of God is a line everyone knew was in his head, but few thought he would dare to write. He referred to the Divine Goodness as:

Whatever brute or blackguard made the world.

Thomas Hardy's disdain of God, and his inordinate desolation—which is the sure symptom of incipient damnation—are put in a more tempered tone. But they are just as irreverent, and quite as blasphemous. Here is Hardy's prayer at a Cathedral Service:

> That with this bright believing band
> I have no claim to be,
> That faiths by which my comrades stand
> Seem fantasies to me,
> And mirage-mists their Shining Land,
> Is a strange destiny.

This plaintive atheism, this irreverent disdain for the minds of those who believe in God, is the heart of Hardy in a nutshell. And as for his soul, it is cold

98

as an English coast, full of treacherous rocks, and seething with surf-like sneers, inviting cheerful light-houses to darken their towers and ships with cargoes of comfort to sail to other ports.

Because he tried with all his might to put one clear and golden cloud in this darkening sky which he saw was coming over his land, we may pay some small tribute here to that elaborately named poet, Dante Gabriel Rossetti, who was born in London, the son of an Italian scholar, an exile. Let it be quite clear, Rossetti was an Italian Protestant, and so his art, from its very start, was a sunset. But he tried once, in the midst of it, in a glorious western sky, with something of the poet Dante's warmth and the Arch-angel Gabriel's respect, to place a bright thought, still lingering from his tradition. It was of a pure Catholic girl, a child of the Blessed Virgin Mary, for whom he coined a London title, "The Blessed Damozel." Here is how she looked as she leaned out from the gold bar of Heaven:

> Her eyes were deeper than the depth
> Of waters stilled at even;
> She had three lilies in her hand,
> And the stars in her hair were seven.

And here is how she lisped when she spoke:

> 'We two,' she said, 'will seek the groves
> Where the lady Mary is,

With her five handmaidens, whose names
  Are five sweet symphonies,
Cecily, Gertrude, Magdalen,
  Margaret and Rosalys.'

These are purely Italian syllables and notes, wedded to purely English notions and names. And that was the last of Rossetti looking for a lady in the sky.

The next Rossetti we know is one who is looking for a lady in a London graveyard. It was the grave of his own wife he was seeking there, a young girl who made hats for London ladies. Rossetti fell in love with this pretty milliner, but because of her delicate health and his own penniless condition, he was unable to marry her until a few months before her tragic death. It was then he did as noble a thing as any poet could do. He buried all his poems in her grave. That was the true Italian in Dante Gabriel Rossetti. The artificial Englishman in him, one is not quite so proud of.

Influenced by a London cult to which he belonged, known as the pre-Raphaelite Movement, and weakened in character because of his association with such superficial aesthetes as William Morris, Burne-Jones, Algernon Charles Swinburne, and eventually that horrid hedonist, Hall Caine, Rossetti was persuaded, for the sake of art, to go back to the London graveyard one night by moonlight, find the coffin of the little milliner's maid, and take out of it the poems he had put there—forever.

And this, I am sad to say, is the end of what I had, or will ever have to say, about D. G. Rossetti.

As I go on speaking of clouds over London, I do not want my reader to think that a cloud in itself is something I abhor. Studied in terms of its own exquisite fabric, it is an item of no small beauty in any sky. I once tried to pay it a tribute in the following soft-textured verse:

THE CLOUD

Song should come promptly when the eye beholds
A Himalaya floating off in folds,
In wayward vales of silent, plume-like lather:
Song should be swift the gist of that to gather,
Have fixed in snow-flame phrases and dispensed
This continent of quiet uncondensed,
Ere the explosion into forks of fire,
The crash and downpour of a frail empire
Whose trickling ruins the minnow shall be fond of
Soon, and paper boats sail on the pond of.

I am not complaining about clouds in their true nature, temporary assignments in the sky, waiting to fall in refreshing and pleasant rain. I am talking against them in the form of obstinate tapestries that do nothing but blot out the sun at those times when the sun was meant to prevail.

I have no particular interest, even, in metaphor-

ical clouds, the kind Queen Victoria—who perpetually sat—looked up at when she saw the constant face
of Benjamin Disraeli. I am not even complaining
against his kind of face. Daniel O'Connell, an
Irish member of Parliament whose specialty was
casting reflections on the complexions of London
peers—who said of one of them that he had "a smile
like the glinting of sunlight on the name-plate of a
coffin"—took extra care in describing the face of
Benjamin Disraeli. O'Connell declared that Disraeli looked like "a lineal descendant of the impenitent thief."

This kind of cloud over London was Queen Victoria's concern, and I do not intend to make it mine.
I prefer to go back to the clouds which obscured the
pure rays of the sun of Revelation—always anxious
to return to a land of instinctive elegance, where blue
eyes and blue skies, blue birds and blue waters, are
singly troubled when any one of these four is missing
in central London, and in its outskirts, which are
England.

Just as light can beget light, so darkness can gener-
ate darkness. In order to know how cloudy was the
thought of some noted London thinker, one is often
required to wait and see how his sons went on
thinking after their father's death. The mind of that
dingy London materialist, Thomas Huxley, is made
most evident to the generation that came after him,

not by what he said himself—either in agreement or disagreement with his associate, Charles Darwin, on points on which they were both monkey minded—but rather in what his descendants, Julian and Aldous Huxley, inherited from their grandfather's impulses in thought, and put into their own writings in the century that followed.

Aldous Huxley preferred licentious thinking to scientific speculation, and wrote books bearing proud titles like, *Grey Eminence* and *Brave New World*. Aldous Huxley was the sentiment of Thomas Huxley set forth by itself. Julian was his sediment, settling at the bottom of a chemistry test tube.

At the end of the world, when nations are judged, and all the true news is told, it will be made clear what a sinister force London, through Julian Huxley, has exercised in the fostering of all that is horrid in twentieth century Russia. Stalin, without British support, could never have stood on his feet. Pavlov, the Russian biologist, making serious sociological experiments in laboratories, would never have been generally accepted unless he had been auspiced by the academic, soft-brutal support of Professor Julian Huxley of England.

I once sat through the showing of a motion picture emanating from Moscow, and edited by London, entitled, "The Mechanics of the Brain." The protagonist in the piece was Pavlov, experimenting on animals and children, and endeavoring to force his audience to see what slight difference there was between them. The experiments were not by way of showing an animal scratching its fleas, and a child saying its prayers. They were all made in the common areas of behavior that seemed to exist among brutes and babies. We were shown the startling similarities of their nerve reactions, saliva secretions, and cerebral tremors. The quiet London voice commenting on all this inductive enlightenment, and approving of it to the last detail, and making inferences which were not supposed to cause us dismay, was the voice of Evolution—Julian Huxley. Mr. Huxley is now in charge of the universal educational program conducted by the United Nations.

The loudest rumbling in large rebellion against the vagaries of the Victorian period was the voice of G. K. Chesterton.

Chesterton is a bulky subject, no matter how you take him. They say he wrote a hundred and fourteen books. I am not prepared to call him a cloud over London, but I think he was something of a cloak over it, and in terms of a cloak I once described him: "In person Chesterton was a large man who was something of a strain on his clothes. Tidiness he persistently ignored in favor of comfort. Everyone who got near him was tempted to rearrange him, or at least to giving thought as to how it could be done. Eventually Chesterton gave up the idea of expecting to be held together in ordinary attire by ordinary threads and buttons, and went around wearing a cloak. The simplicity with which one could secure a sort of stylish seclusion by the tying of a single knot or the fastening of a single hook appealed to Chesterton. A cloak was a garment calculated to reveal not how he was fashioned, but where he was to be found."

Chesterton, though he makes constant protest of needing the supernatural in moral life, never gives any indication of needing it in dogmatic thought. He gives the definite impression that he could have reached most of the revealed values of the Gospel with his own powers of discovery, and have written them down to his own satisfaction with his own vast abilities of utterance. Almost everything he quotes from Holy Scripture he does so by way of improving on it. He says in one place that even if he never heard of original sin, he could have discovered it for himself.

G. K. Chesterton wrote a book called *Heretics* in 1904, in which he disavowed all attachment to Protestantism. He wrote another book called *Orthodoxy* in 1906, in which he affirmed his allegiance to Catholicism. It took him sixteen more years—until 1922—before he lifted himself from an overcomfortable armchair, and walked, puffing, into a Catholic chapel to make the required profession of faith and submit to the ceremony of conversion. This scandalous delay in coming into the fold of Christ, never seems to have caused Chesterton any regrets. He seems glad to have given the impression that he did not allow himself to be rushed.

Chesterton's style of thinking and writing was far too colossal for Christianity. I put him in parody, once, on the nursery rhyme, "Rock-a-bye Baby." Here is the colossal way in which he would commence:

> He sways on the topmost branches,
> Encradled in purple gloom,
> The child too high for the hilltop
> The child too large for the room.

Anyone looking for the Babe of Bethlehem at Christmas time—either by way of regal wisdom or rural simplicity, as a king following a star, as a shepherd listening to a song—had better avoid the books of G. K. Chesterton. There is altogether too much of Christianity in them, and altogether too little of Christ. If I may reverse a proverb of Omar Khayyám, Chesterton was one who "took the credit and let the cash go."

Hilaire Belloc, whose favorite recreation all during middle life was riding on the top of London busses and looking at cloudy skies, had good reasons for this forlorn form of recreation. His has been an almost lifelong loneliness, caused by the loss of a young wife, only a few years after he married her.

Her death put in him a heartache that never let
him love again.

Hilaire Belloc is a Londoner in looks, a Londoner
in walk and talk, and a Londoner in stubbornness.
But he is the only London writer I know—with the
possible exception of Philip Guedalla—who is not a
Londoner in soul. Belloc has a Continental soul—a
perfect sympathy with things French, Austrian
and Italian, and a perfect shrewdness for everything
that is German. Belloc never lost his Continental
kinship with soldiers (he once served in the army of
France), nor did he ever lose his sense of comrade-
ship with the spirits of Continental saints, nearly
every one of whose shrines he has at some time visited, making the journey on foot. His is also a Continental thirst for wine.

Belloc refuses to drink any liquor discovered or
invented since the Protestant Reformation. The
odors of brandy, sherry and port delight his Catholic
sense of smell, but whiskey is a word one must never
utter in his presence. I am almost afraid to put it in
a paragraph where the name of Belloc is mentioned.

As I write these lines, Hilaire Belloc is himself
in a cloud. He is now an old man, older, as he once
remarked, than the Little Flower of Jesus would be
were she still alive. Belloc has now a bent back, is
helpless, is unshaven, is unreliable in all his remembrances, and faithful only to his memories. He sits
by the fireside in some hidden country place, and

waits for the tap on the shoulder that is to be his summons to the Particular Judgment.

When Belloc goes to Purgatory—I am positive Our Lord will never send him to Hell—I know he will be required to purge his soul of some of the interests collected there during life, by reason of too much association, even in the heat of conflict, with some of the heretics of his time. But I also believe he will be promised high rewards in Heaven for the clear courage with which he proclaimed all central Catholic truths, fearless of what would be the consequence to himself.

Two or three of Belloc's poems are already assuredly immortal, and this is a good deal to have achieved in any single lifetime.

I think perhaps the poem of Belloc's which deserves to be best known, after his death, is that knightly masterpiece written in defense of a little serving-maid, who, in her disgrace, was being curtailed by the cruelty of a Queen. This little serving-maid is the type of England's perpetual girl, when left to her own longing. She is lonely for Our Blessed Lady. She is figuratively buried from the kitchen of a palace where she has drooped and died of heartbreak.

> Great lords carried her,
> And proud priests prayed,
> And that was the end
> Of the little serving-maid.

The last four poets laureate of England have been named, respectively: Alfred, Alfred, Robert and John. It was after the regime of the first and second Alfreds—Alfred Tennyson, who was all poet and no laureate, and Alfred Austin, who was all laureate and no poet—that an enterprising young Londoner named Alfred Noyes made an overture for the job himself. It was by way of writing London an epic poem, called "Drake," which purported to be in the nature of a Virgilian laudation of the British Empire, somewhat in the manner in which Aeneas has been used as a symbol of the anticipated glories of Rome.

Unfortunately, however, Alfred Noyes failed to impress the committee that chooses London's poet laureate, and the award was made to Robert Bridges, who wrote, while in office, a long, tiresome poem called "A Testament to Beauty," and left orders in his will that his body be cremated and no biography of himself be written. So, perhaps I had better leave him immediately, and get back to the rejected candidate, Alfred Noyes.

I do not know any poet in modern London who was more entitled to the award of poet laureate than Alfred Noyes. His lighter lyrics, such as "The Highwayman" and "Come Down to Kew in Lilac Time," have been as charming and memorable as any recent verses I know. When Noyes found that London did not like him as much as he wanted it to, he emigrated to America in 1913, and taught English literature at Princeton University.

Princeton University has a way of attracting Englishmen on visits, which Harvard and Yale never seem to be able to acquire. I think Englishmen feel that Harvard and Yale are competitors in New England of Oxford and Cambridge in the England that is old. Princeton, they feel, is quite out of the running, and therefore a safe place to visit and condescend to.

However, Princeton University, on one occasion, gave London a snub, which was more than well warranted. It was given by two young Princeton students standing one evening in the University's railroad station. The story is a classic, and deserves to be put into imperishable archives.

London has had, in its history, two men named Walter Raleigh. The one was a knight in Queen Elizabeth's time. The other has been knighted in our present day. The former was knighted for his courtesy, and the latter for his competence at letters. This second Sir Walter Raleigh, the knight of our own day, was traveling down to Princeton one evening from New York, to give a lecture. He arrived on the train after the one he had been expected to take. There was no kindly lecture committee waiting in the station to receive him—only two Princeton students, who had not the slightest notion who he was, or even that he was expected to come there at all.

Sir Walter Raleigh, upon getting off the train, and finding no one to meet him, went up to these students and said:

"Could you please tell me where is Princeton University? I am Sir Walter Raleigh."

"Oh, good evening, Sir Walter," said one of the students, as he made a profound bow. "And this," he said, pointing to his companion, "is the Earl of Essex. And I," he said, pointing to himself, "am Sir Christopher Blount. And you will find Queen Elizabeth at the moment, smoking cigarettes in the men's room."

Alfred Noyes soon grew tired of Princeton, and returned to London. He soon grew tired of everything Anglican, including the Anglican Church. It was then that he was converted to the Roman Catholic Church. His conversion he kept quiet for nearly two years, perhaps so as to see if it were genuine. I have suspicions that it was not. Not because of the two years in which he failed to profess his Faith, but because of two books he has written since openly admitting his religious allegiance. The one is called *The Unknown God,* in which, it is claimed, that Jesus Christ, with arms outstretched on the Cross is the fruit of Evolution as it reached the summit of the progress for which it was intended; and the second, is a sympathetic biography of that French blasphemer, *Voltaire.*

Elsewhere, in London's sky, on sunny days (which I call the days when poets are being inspired—even Robert Browning said, "Oh, to be in England, now that April's there!")—are (a) a family of poets called the Sitwells, and (b) a clique of poets which I may call the "W. H. Audenites."

The Sitwells are two brothers and a sister—Osbert, Sacheverell, and Edith. The best of the three, I am pleased to say, is Edith; just as the best of New York's poetic family, the Benéts—William Rose, Stephen Vincent and Laura—is Laura, the one still living, for whom, because of some almost Mary-sweet utterances in her earlier work, I constantly pray.

The Audenites are more of a problem. In a poem called "Song for a Listener," I combine Spender, Auden and Eliot into a single name. I call him "Spoundel." And here is the verse I have on him:

> Because his lyre was newly strung,
> Because the poet still was young,
> One read some lines that Spoundel sung;
>
> And found that what he thought untoward
> He wallowed in, and thanked the Lord
> He was not bored with being bored,—
>
> And made elliptical allusions
> To obfuscate his own confusions
> And ostracize his own exclusions.

Roy Campbell, a kind of a cowboy Catholic poet, now living in London, thought this idea of grouping

the obscurantists into one name a good one. By way
of sheer plagiarism from me, he called Louis Mac-
Niece, Stephen Spender, W. H. Auden and C. Day
Lewis, grouped into one man, "MacSpoundey."
Under this name we may dismiss them.

The one poet in this list above who is going, not
merely to be damned for his beliefs, but to receive
extra punishment in Hell for abusing his abilities,
is W. H. Auden. Two slight flashes of his latent
powers are enough to indicate his responsibility
for his talent. They are (a) by way of putting Hor-
ace's censure upon an overpraiser of the past in this
form:

> Let us honor if we can
> The vertical man,
> Although we value none
> But the horizontal one

which is the wisest geometry I know; but also (b) for
saying in another stanza of three lines more than
many a thriftier poet says in three hundred.

> Private faces in public places
> Are wiser and nicer
> Than public faces in private places

which means you would rather meet your next-door
neighbor in Buckingham Palace, than meet Mahatma Gandhi in your bath.

T. S. Eliot is not a cloud over London. He is a cloud in it. He does not hide the light of the sun there. He confuses those who are looking for it.

T. S. Eliot is a Royalist in politics, a Classicist in literature, an Anglo-Catholic in religion, and a London taxpayer by request. He was formerly an American. He was born and bred in St. Louis, Missouri, and acquired later cultivation in Boston, Massachusetts. It is hard to imagine more alienation, snobbery, heresy, disloyalty—in a word, more mongrelism in any one man's credentials. He is a synthetic surprise no country can fully claim, no culture be fully blamed for.

> Polyphiloprogenitive
> The sapient sutlers of the Lord
> Drift across the window-panes

is T. S. Eliot's unintelligible way of saying that bugs on windows are rapid breeders. "Murder in the Cathedral" is his mid-Western American manner of referring to the martyrdom of a London saint.

I once sat opposite T. S. Eliot at a dinner, where he made a sincere effort at being sincere, and a modest effort at being modest, all during the meal. I later put this sapient sutler in a verse, which I entitled, "Reflection on a Flea." I shall omit its beginning and its end. Here is how it continues:

> I loathe the aesthetic attitude,
> The literary languish,

The anguish after anguish,
The hunger for hunger, not for food,—
The joy that is not jolly,
The making tears a trade,
The professional melancholy,
The fear of being afraid.
I hide my whole head under
The sheets when I hear thunder.
Things, and not theories,
Frighten and make me freeze.
And, by the way,
Speaking of how to pray,
Dogmas come first, not liturgies.
The dilettante hand,
That took art seriously,
That outlawed fairyland
And stripped the Christmas tree,
Now tries another trick,
And has revived Our Lord
To go with the candle-stick
It has so long adored.
Of faith it finds a clue
In hyphenated points of view,
Whose novelty is never new,
And whose waste-land has got
A penny watering-pot
Filled up with drops of dew.

A doubt is still a doubt,
Even turned inside out.

I may speak, at this point, of a distant cloud that has lately tried to descend on London from the north-west. It has come down from the cold mountains of Northern Ireland, where the doubters dwell. His name is C. S. Lewis.

C. S. Lewis begins his theology, not with Heaven and God, but with Hell and Lucifer. He pretends that this Lucifer is a theological distillation of what one finds in the whole field of Christian dogma, when it is carefully studied.

C. S. Lewis has taken upon himself the task of helping the Protestant heresies to get rid of their nostalgias. He ends up by declaring in favor of some Catholic dogmas, but not any Catholic dogmatists; against all Protestant heresies, but very much for some Protestant heretics. His purpose is always a super-clear conclusion. He considers the clarity of focus in attention to be the covenanted clarity of the Faith. He has no vision, but most intense powers of observation. He notes with especial care, what large victories the Devil is scoring in unbelieving England by way of gluttony. His glutton is a little English spinster, altogether too fussy about her tea, and wanting too much butter on her toast.

Lewis does not dislike snakes. He is a member of the Society for the Prevention of Cruelty to Animals, for which he has written doctrinal treatises. His is a cosmological theology, in which angelology and zoology are given appropriate and proportionate attention. He has one sentence to say about the Queen of Angels. She is referred to as the one "who presumably conceived Christ without sin."

A charming and competent American woman, Clare Boothe Luce, who has had experience at writing plays, was invited a few years ago to collaborate with C. S. Lewis in the making of a motion picture on the subject of the Devil. It was to be called "Screwtape." It was to be all Lucifer, and no Blessed Lady. All snake, and no precious heel—promised to crush him, in the third chapter of Genesis.

I wrote to Clare Boothe Luce, to protest against this partnership, and against this picture. My protest may or may not have been the reason why the project was abandoned. But here is what I said to Clare when I urged her to give Lewis the gate:

> If Lucifer were a Lewis affair,
> Do you think C. S. would take
> Such charming, literary care
> Of a snake?
>
> And if Lucifer were a Luce affair,
> Do you think Clare Boothe would feel
> Afraid to step on him head and hair
> With her heel?

And now for two or three more clouds coming down on London from the north, and then I am through with London clouds.

Monsignor Ronald Knox is the son of an Anglican bishop and the brother of an Anglican minister.
He severed his own connections with Anglicanism
so as to acquire the central assurances and valid
orders of Rome. His change of religious allegiance
was managed without any apparent ruffling of his
relatives, and he entered the Church, pipe in hand.
That pipe he has not since put down, not even in
photographs. Nor has he put aside any of his former
canniness and nimble ability to amuse. Chesterton
paid him a compliment for this in a quatrain:

> Mary of Holyrood must smile indeed,
> Knowing what grim, historic shade it shocks,
> To see wit, laughter and the Popish creed
> Cluster and sparkle in the name of Knox.

One day, in a room full of beer fumes and tobacco
smoke, a young university student said to Monsignor
Knox, "Ronnie! What is a good definition of an egotist?"

"An egotist," Monsignor Knox replied, puffing
away at his pipe, "is one who won't let you talk
about yourself."

Monsignor Knox is famous for such witticisms.
And here is a specimen of his spiritual wisdom.

Life, says Monsignor Knox—by way of proposing
a parable—may be compared to an examination we
all must take in order to get into Heaven. The saints
are taking this examination for honors, the rest of us

for pass degrees. And God will be glad to pass all of us, provided we do not disturb the saints while they are taking their examinations.

This Knoxian version of "The Laborers in the Vineyard" might be called "The Loafers in the Classroom."

Ronald Knox is a great one for knowing the boundaries of things, both in behavior and in thought. And he has a shrewd way of keeping the apostle and the apologete in a priest, distinct. One is in doubt at times as to whether he wants England to come back to the Church, or the Church to come back to England. I once heard him say, when he was the Catholic chaplain at Oxford, that his purpose there was not to make conversions, but only to minister to those who already had the Faith. His own reasons for becoming a Catholic—his previous wide reading and proficiency in the humanities, his spiritual indebtedness to Virgil's "Aeneid"—most of the students were familiar with, thanks to his many books and articles on the subject. Some of the students, however, thought Monsignor Knox's logic too tactful to be innocently true, and they felt that if he stopped his affirmative arguments for a moment, and polished up his negative premises, he might easily win on the other side.

Monsignor Knox, by way of revising the bad English of the Church he entered, recently loaned it his vocabulary, and issued an edition of Holy Scripture known as "The Knox Bible." In this Bible, Ronald Knox figuratively puts wrist watches on all the Evangelists, and invites them to dinner in a don's refectory, where, in the midst of revelation and refreshment, they may be colloquially introduced, and may receive academic credit for being the excellent and inspired authors they are.

Monsignor Knox has also lately written a doctrinal divertissement, a light piece, known as *The Mass in Slow Motion*. In it we learn, among other things, the reason why the priest turns round at the Offertory to say the *Orate Fratres*. It is to wake up the altar boys who have been sleeping while his back was turned. There being now no Chesterton to add a quatrain to this incident, I should like to add one of my own.

> Mary of Holyrood must weep indeed
> Knowing what immemorial saints it shocks,
> To see Mass measured at a movie speed
> And offered to Hollywood in the name of Knox.

At Oxford, in England, when I visited it, Monsignor Knox was first among the Roman Catholic intellectuals. His closest competitor was a member of a religious order, a semicelebrity whose name, though simple, is easily misspelled, and which I therefore avoid, but whose studiously uncut hair and studiously oversized clothes I still loosely remember, and who has always reminded what is undergraduate in me of a turkey in profile, gargling a golf ball, and clerical-collared with a quoit.

Among Monsignor Knox's non-competitors, but on the list of his recurrent callers, was Mr. Evelyn (pronounced Evil-in) Waugh, whose father, a London publisher, supplied his sons with early printing privileges in pornography, before one of them (Evelyn) turned to hagiography, and whitened his sepulchre with the life of a saint.

VI

CHILD IN THE LONDON STREETS

The child in the London streets is not just any stray child in a large city. He is not the Greek *paidarion;* precious with unregenerated eagerness, impetuous in appetite for the lost apples of Paradise.

The child in the London streets is not the child in the avenues of Berlin, dwarfed by adult ideas. Nor is he the child in the squares of Rome, doomed to adult destinies. He is not even the child in the boulevards of Paris, dismissed in adult arrangements.

London's child is the child of the simple thoroughfare, the child who belongs to a place. The very sidewalks of his city have been measured for his footsteps. He can run down one well-known London lane in the very time it takes to say an Our Father. This brief byway is London's Paternoster Row. At the end of it comes Amen Corner, where he must not forget to say "Amen." I suspect that even London's Fleet Street was named after running children.

The London child, during the period in which he is listening to language, and learning how to think, is a little knight in a Kingdom not of this world—for he is almost never not baptized. One Christian Sacrament London still clings to, and to the preserved little dresses and bonnets that go with it. And that is the Sacrament of Baptism.

Now, there are not many Baptisms—a Baptism in the true Church of Christ, and other baptisms in the churches of the heresies. There is only one Baptism. Whoever receives this Baptism, is given all it was meant to impart, provided he puts no obstacle in the way—a thing a young child is incapable of doing. And so, the child in the London streets is, almost certainly, a little son of God—about to be cheated, alas, by unbelieving elders, of all the rest of his supernatural heritage.

Were the London child to die before refusing his second Sacrament, the Sacrament of the Bread of Life, and for which his Baptism was a divine preparation, he would go to Heaven, as an adopted son of God. And this is the Church's clear teaching.

There are millions of such London children in Heaven. Their titles to beatitude were in spirit, not in flesh. They have stolen in by reason of their sanctified innocence—*non Angli, sed Angeli*—to steal a phrase from St. Gregory the Great.

My reader now knows my intolerant feeling about all little London boys and girls; and if I may use this bigotry as a background, I think I can interpret them as they deserve to be known.

The child in the London streets is not taught very much by grown-ups. Most of what he knows he has had to teach himself. No one, for instance, can tell you where his favorite nursery rhymes come from. They seem to have been evoked out of nowhere, handed on by children to children, from generation to generation. Whenever a London adult has gone out of his way to publish, in Fleet Street, a book of rhymes for a London child, it has almost never reached a child who will read it. It is kept on the shelves of London's fashionable clubs, and chuckled over by a lot of bibulous old boys when they are potted.

The London child is a wonderfully self-sustained little waif, with an imagination whetted for the conquest of anything. Jumping over the moon seems too easy. So he gives this assignment to a clumsy cow. The killing of giants, however, he views with respect, and keeps this as one of his own special privileges.

The London child has a marvelous sense of the sounds of things. Standing on a street corner, at Angelus time, in silence, and listening to the bells in a church tower ring, he manages, by a fascinating mixture of noises, to give exactly the music of what the bells are saying:

> Oranges and lemons
> Sing the bells of St. Clemens.

No child in the streets of any other European city was ever more delightfully inventive.

The child in the London streets loves approximate, rather than accurate, sounds in his songs. But so, indeed, does God, in the music of nature—in the breezes of the trees, the ripples of the waters, and the chirpings of the birds.

Rhymes which are correct, just for their own sake, never please the London child. He does not deliberately avoid good rhymes. He simply does not care whether or not they occur, as long as you are pleased with the tones of what he is telling you. He defends the pussy-cat with a rhyme like this:

> Who never did him any harm
> But killed the mice in his father's barn.

He tells a Rock-a-bye-baby that:

> On the tree top
> The cradle will rock.

He lets Jack and Jill ascend and descend a hill together, as perfect companions in everything, except rhyme.

> To fetch a pail of water

was the way they both went up;

> And Jill came tumbling after

was how one of them came down.

Only a happy child could put together such unmatched sounds with such confident assurance and lyrical delight. You feel that these little rhymes match about as much as patches on his breeches, or buttons on his shirt.

Psychological historians of recent times have assigned deep, adult meanings to many of London's nursery rhymes.

> The King was in the countinghouse,
> Counting up his money

they tell us, was Henry VIII.

> The Queen was in the parlour,
> Eating bread and honey

was Catherine of Aragon.

> The maid was in the garden
> Hanging out the clothes

was Anne Boleyn.

> Along came a black bird
> And snipped off her nose

was an ecclesiastic from the Diocesan Matrimonial Court, who warned her that she must not break up a royal and valid marriage.

The study of London's nursery rhymes has been given much importance recently in some American universities. Theses are written on them so as to secure graduate degrees in the fields of psychology and political science. I think it ought to be noted, however, that (a) political nursery rhymes are not the ones that London children really love; and (b) the creators of them must have been listening to the rhythms of children in the streets so as to know how good cadences go.

I have often wanted to take some of these nursery rhymes, which the scholars have not yet decoded, and offer a few good guesses of my own. Could it be that:

> Baa, baa, black sheep
> Have you any wool?

meant

> Are there any more Cardinal Wolseys
> Among the clergy?

Could it be that:

> This is the malt that lay
> In the House that Jack built

meant

The refreshment that Londoners are likely to miss
In John Milton's *Paradise Lost?*

Frankly, if this last were true, even I would be driven back to the morbid wisdom of A. E. Housman, when he said:

And malt does more than Milton can
To justify God's ways to man.

Not only are the nursery rhymes of the London child the fruit of some unestablished authorship—part child and part parent, lodged together God knows where, collaborating God knows how—but it is to be noted that both in London and in all its surrounding towns, to no one does an adult speak with more careful exactitude or more enunciated respect than he does when speaking to a child.

Childishness, in London, is not a characteristic of children. But it is of grown-ups. When situations get too intense for London grownups, they violently turn to simplicities. The poor betake themselves to a cinema, or a pub, and act skittishly for the rest of the evening. The less poor go off to a music hall, and listen to a Gilbert and Sullivan opera, the most childish entertainment ever seriously produced.

The London child begins life, as I have said, with a Christian challenge in his eyes. This purity of gaze annoys the skepticism of his elders, and so, as his years advance, he is kept from believing lots of things he would like to.

Disgusting experiments on London children have recently been made in the name of pediatrics. Lord Bertrand Russell has been one of the most realistic of these experimenters. The uneducated English child kept torturing the conscience of this impurely educated Englishman. And so, Russell started a school for children, with a curriculum that would do credit to a stable. He put this school in the country. The children were exposed to all temptations, and encouraged to settle them in terms of their own instincts. No counsel or correction was allowed to be given them. It was a school where impulses were fostered, and noted, and statistics constantly kept.

Lord Russell was forced to close this school. The children had turned into savages. Light begets light. Darkness generates darkness. The offspring of a demon are little devils in the flesh.

In the field of supposedly polite education, we have the English public school. English writers have let us know that these public schools are not good. Dickens went out of his way to say so. Shelley shrieked it. Any graduate of these schools will quietly admit it, if you can get him to give you his confidence.

The child in an English public school is a darling little boy, put into long trousers long before his time. He is learning how to hold his head high by way of mastery over himself. He is learning how to try not to let anyone know the disappointments that he feels in his soul. He calls his parents, in Anglicized Latin, "Pater" and "Mater." He greets them almost with a salute. He knows he must stand on his own two feet, more than any poor mortal was ever intended to. The Empire may need him, so he must prepare for banishment. The local offices of the Kingdom may require him, so he must set himself for slavery.

The public-school boy of London, and of greater England, must ignore disappointment and disillusionment, and meet all disasters with a smile. It is only the least-paid servant in his house who knows the secrets of his heart. It is on her shoulder that he buries his head, in some hidden seclusion, where he may weep, and weep, and weep.

The Catholic public schools of England have not made much improvement on this Protestant public-school arrangement. Catholics have no universities in England, but of public schools they have a number.

These Catholic public schools—in America they would be called private schools—are always anxious to let the Ministers of Education see, that, though Catholic beliefs are alien to what London generally holds, Catholic customs can be kept in conformity with the practice of the majority. Boys in Catholic schools are still flogged, because flogging is an accepted public-school discipline. The manners and terminologies in England's Catholic schools are rarely illustrative of any of the truths of the Faith. Every Catholic public school feels singularly honored when one of its graduates is accepted for Oxford or for Cambridge.

There was a time when the Vatican forbade English Catholic boys to go to Oxford or to Cambridge. When the English hierarchy secured permission for this to be done, the Vatican was somewhat reluctant to give in. But modern England has a way of influencing the Vatican. Everyone in London speaks of this. Everyone in Rome whispers it. For the sake of a share in British prestige, the Vatican is anxious not to displease England.

The letter of permission from the Vatican allowing English boys to attend Protestant universities contained a warning. It purported to have come from the Pope. He said, "I send you as sheep in the midst of wolves." This is a new version of an old parable— the parable of the Good Shepherd.

Perhaps some of these animadversions I make on the London child are the fruit of heartaches I had, walking in the London streets. It was for two years I did so, when I was a young priest. And here is how I mused, as I walked, in a verse called simply,

The Children

When I go out walking
   On Bloomsbury Street,
Children say "Here he comes!"
   Children I meet;

The Margarets and Marys
   And Michaels and Matts,

131

Dropping me curtseys
  And lifting their hats.

The children! The children!
  They load me with love,
In Bloomsbury Gardens
  And Bloomsbury Grove.

By Bloomsbury Chapel
  And Bloomsbury Mart,
I often go walking
  To kindle my heart.

But, when I go out walking
  On Buckingham Lane,
Children say "Here he comes
  Walking again."

The Gladyses, Gwendolyns,
  Grovers and Guys,
Lifting their noses
  And arching their eyes.

The children! The children!
  They hurt me with hate,
In Buckingham Terrace
  And Buckingham Gate.

By Buckingham Mansions
  And Buckingham Inns,
I often go walking
  To pay for my sins.

In the last one hundred years, while the skeptical London mind has kept thwarting the London child, the worst tyrants have not always been those who have had charge of him in public schools. They were very often the parents he met when he returned for a holiday, whose adult playful interests never matched his serious thoughts. His *pater* and *mater*—by way of offering him homestead pleasantry—could give him phrases from *The Rivals,* and quotations from a play called *Lady Windermere's Fan.* In the books of his father's library, he found nothing that could nourish the needs of his soul. Obviously not the insipid novels of J. M. Barrie, who was the namby-pamby boy in his own books. And the situation was just as bad in books for girls.

There was once a little girl named Liddell. Her father was a famous London lexicographer—of the team of Liddell & Scott. An older friend of hers was a popular Protestant minister, who for the sake, perhaps, of modesty, started writing under a pseudonym. This Protestant minister called himself Lewis Carroll; and he put Miss Liddell in a book. He called her Alice; and the book in which he put her he called, *Alice in Wonderland.* There was only one thing wrong with the book. Little Miss Liddell did not especially care for it. She never understood that, when Reverend Mr. Carroll was writing, it was she who was supposed to be speaking.

I do not know where this tragic London child of the Nineteenth Century ended in literature. Perhaps in the *Beau Geste* novels of Sir Percival Christopher Wren. One place, I know, where there is not a hint of him is in the *Christopher Robin* of A. A. Milne. And I may mention two other places where there is not even a hint of his ever having existed. It is in the adulterous fiction of John Galsworthy, and in the superannuated dramas of G. B. Shaw.

If my reader wants to remember the anguish of the child I am trying to commemorate, let him avoid all the routine childrens' books: *A Kiss for Cinderella* and *Peter Pan*. Let him stand, some quiet evening, beneath a London church tower, whose bells are commencing to ring, and let him repeat:

> Oranges and lemons
> Sing the bells of St. Clemens.

And then he will probably know what temporary treasures are still skipping ropes and rolling hoops in the foggy London streets.

VII

HYDE PARK

In the days of horses, before busses came along, traffic in London's Piccadilly progressed at a rate of speed which varied from six to eight miles an hour. The speed at which you may now expect to ride, in a cab or a tram, from Piccadilly Circus to Trafalgar Square, from Oxford Circus to the Bank of England, is from four to six miles an hour. One would never have thought the automobile could have so slowed London down.

London's streets were not meant for the automobile. Automobile, may I add, is a forbidden English noun. It is mongrel in origin—part Latin, and part Greek—*autos* from the Greek and *mobile* from the Latin. No London grammarian would invent such a word, no London pedagogue award it his approval.

What New York calls *automobile,* London must refer to as *motor car*. And *motor car* it goes on being called, even though it pauses as much as it progresses through the crowded and curious-shaped London streets.

London's streets were made for persons, and not for machines. I think it nice that these streets are named, and not numbered.

Hurry in London is not good for one. There is much to miss if you pass too quickly. Let us take, for instance, London's Saints, and the Spots to which their names still cling.

London's Saints are saints only in Heaven and in London. They are the private possessions of the Popes who may have canonized them, and the places from which they were presented. Here are some of their names, which are strange at first hearing, but as familiar to London as the stones in its pavements:

St. Marylebone, St. Pancras, St. Giles, St. Bartholomew-the-Great, St. Vidast, St. Olaves, St. Andrew-on-the-Wall, St. Magnus, St. Benet, St. Mary Le Bow, St. Mary Abchurch, St. Mary Aldermary, St. Katherine-of-the-Docks.

If anyone doubts this litany, let him take a walk— or even a ride—through London, and these names will be staring him in the face. "God help us!" is an ejaculation heard everywhere in London. "Pray for us!" could be another, anywhere you look.

A Cross and a Sword underneath the helmet of a knight, displayed between two dragons, over the words "Domine Dirige Nos" is—God help us!—the coat-of-arms of the City of London.

Another signature of the preciousness of London as a place, is the list of gates that enfold it. Every small section of this aging metropolis seems to be jealously guarded behind its own especial gate. There is:

Aldgate, Bishopsgate, Moorgate and Aldersgate; St. John's Gate, Cripplegate, Queensgate, and Ludgate near St. Paul's.

Where gates seem too large or seem prohibitive, courts move in and surround:

Earl's Court, Tottenham Court, Hampton Court; Grosvenor Court, and, of course, The Court of the King.

The rest of London's structures, solicitous for privacy, are called palladiums, palaces, hospitals, hotels, embassies, galleries, museums, towers, halls, inns, castles, and jails.

The London bobbies, who act as traffic guardians, coldly give information to inquirers. They assume that everything in London is intimate and familiar, even to visitors from foreign lands. Whether it be Bird Cage Walk, or Madame Tussaud's. Whether it be Pickle Street, Herring Street, or Traitors' Gate.

137

Whether it be The Apothecaries', Nelson's Column, or Cleopatra's Needle. Whether The Cenotaph, Bush House, Selfridge's, Peter Robinson's, The Wallace Collection, The Brownings', or, The Portuguese Consulate. Every London bobby knows these occupancies down to the last inch, and will immediately tell one how to go there, and point in the right direction.

After making a general survey of all of London's enclosures—its squares, its gardens, its arboretums, and its conservatories—in brief, after somehow remembering all its varieties of place, each of them signatured with a special name and asserted to be the like of which you will never see again, it is nice to find, not far from the center of London, a wide space large enough for everyone to roam in; where one can sleep in the shade, lunch under the trees, or swim in a clear, cool stream. It is the place where London squirrels abound, and skylarks ascend for their ecstatic songs. It is where Londoners went for duels in the days when duels were permitted. It is where speakers, with messages to give the world, now stand upon boxes, which are called "pitches," and orate to audiences and gesticulate to the sky.

A beautiful portico entitled Marble Arch is the most official entrance to the great place I am now describing. A boundary that protects it is a stretch-

way of flowers, called Kensington Gardens. An ave-
nue that leads from it is named Rotten Row, perhaps
to let one know the excellence of area from which
one is departing, when one steps out of the precincts
of—Hyde Park.

Hyde Park is a rendezvous for the middle-aged
and the old. Children do come there, but are usually
brought by parents. Lovers also walk there, but
dislike being over-observed. Personages promenade
there, for the sake of air or exercise, or maybe, even,
for a change of point of view. But the middle-aged
and the elderly are the ones always found there,
seated on benches, or lying on the grass. It is they
who are the inhabitants of Hyde Park.

One old man, sitting on a bench, says to another
old man beside him, while pointing to a third old
man across the way,

"He has about as much brains as a dickie-bird!"

And you marvel at the fluttering delicacy of this criticism.

One old woman, with her Sunday coat on, and
who has forgotten to take off her apron, says—maybe
to someone, maybe to no one; perhaps half to herself,
and half to the sky—"I wonder how God keeps track
of us all, there's such a thumpin' lot of us."

Two limeys are sitting on another bench, and arguing about an accident.

Says one: "Don't you tell me there's a God in heaven. Lettin' a fine man like that be smashed down by a motor car. Don't you tell me there is, after that!"

"Now you look here, Colcord," says the other, "you're gettin' it wrong. Don't you forget, God never makes a mistake."

"Come to think of it, you're right!" says Colcord. "I never looked at it that way before. Thank you very much, dear Abercrombie. Thank you very much for tellin' me."

A somewhat handsome man, with splendid fabric in his clothes, and a semi-majestic girl—trying to keep up with him, stride for stride—are passing down The Ring Road. Somebody tells you—and then you recognize—that they are Jack Hurlburt and Cicely Courtneidge, London's best and bravest comedians.

Jack Hurlburt and Cicely Courtneidge are the only English actors, as far as I know, whom Hollywood has been unable to lure away from London, and New York unable to coax away from the Strand. This was not because they were not funny enough to go to America. There were no acts in American vaudeville that could approach them in silly delightfulness, or in complete and competent charm.

It was for selfish reasons they refused to cross the ocean. Environment was part of their powers of entertainment, and they did not want to sacrifice it and ruin their art.

One remembers what tragedies occurred in the lives of other London comedians when they tried to be funny away from their milieu. Everybody knows how weirdly Gracie Fields began to screech when she transferred to the Palace in New York. Everyone has sensed what disillusionment crept into the face of Gertrude Lawrence when she gave up Mayfair for Manhattan. Londoners have wept to see Beatrice Lillie (Lady Peel) cast her pearls before Bronx and Brooklyn. And there never was a case of a shattering of bright abilities equal to the freeze-out given to Reginald Gardiner, when his precious humors were transported to Broadway.

Reginald Gardiner used to say that there were two kinds of windshield wipers—a short kind which went fast, a long kind which went slow. The short one kept saying:

"Wooden shoe, Wooden shoe, Wooden shoe,"

the long one,

"Beef tea, Beef tea, Beef tea."

But, to go back to Mr. Hurlburt and Miss Courtneidge. Hyde Park is proud of an actor and an actress who kept all their skits in the places where they belong; and who are increasingly appreciated the older they grow; and who have never been disillusioned with the art of being amusing; and who have never failed to amuse those meant to appreciate them.

London is a place. And it never had a joke that left it and continued to be funny.

I once sat in a London cinema, with a Londoner, watching an American movie. In it were the four Marx Brothers. I spent half my time looking at this picture, and half my time explaining to my companion what the Marx Brothers were up to.

Here was a Marx Brother situation I found very hard to explain:

Groucho Marx: "You remind me of a man by the name of Emmanuel Ravelli."

Chico Marx: "I *am* Emmanuel Ravelli."

Groucho Marx: "Well, no wonder you look alike."

(They pause)

Groucho Marx: "But I still insist there is a resemblance."

My London companion took hold of my wrist, in a dark theatre, and pleaded for an explanation.

My Companion: "What did Groucho make that last remark for?"

142

Myself: "To make the situation absurd."

My Companion: "But wasn't the situation sufficiently absurd before he made that remark?"

Myself: "I suppose it was. But Americans have a theory about absurd situations."

My Companion: (pleadingly) "And what is that?"

Myself: "They consider no absurd situation ever sufficiently absurd."

On one of the benches in Hyde Park sits a proud proverb-maker. He does not offer a new proverb too frequently. But there is one old one he keeps constantly repeating. And he seems able to apply it to almost any situation that may arise. How he does this, when I am away from him, I never can quite recall. But when seated beside him, I seem always convinced. I am convinced that what is wrong with our modern civilization is that most of us fail to remember that (and here is his proverb *de luxe*):

"It's not the 'orses' shoes that 'urt the 'orses' 'ooves; it's the constant pitter-patter on the 'ard, 'ard 'ighway; that's what 'urts the 'orses' 'ooves."

Another bloke spends most of his time standing, leaning with his elbow against a tree. He is constantly letting those around him know how quickly things can occur; how swiftly changes happen, even in world affairs. It is all summarized in the following reference-rate. It is:

"Before you could say tit-willow!"

A pleasant day turned into rain—"before you could say tit-willow!" A man was rich, and then became poor—"before you could say tit-willow!" Hitler was running things, but one day he crashed—"before you could say tit-willow!" Even England's Empire, if she didn't look out would tragically disintegrate, or else fold up—"before you could say tit-willow!"

Political arguments on Hyde Park benches are always interesting, too, especially when someone, without standing up, keeps squirming around with rage or excitement. I once heard a man complain against Prime Minister Ramsay MacDonald:

"He makes my bleed, my blood, my boil!"

Shortly afterwards, Ramsay MacDonald was removed from office—before you could say tit-willow!

On a corner of a bench that is under a tree, old Mr. Flintlock sits. If somebody happens to be sitting beside him, he gives this somebody a lecture. If nobody happens to be seated beside him, he whispers this lecture to himself. Once I sat beside him for nearly an hour, and I should very much like,

144

here, to pay him my respects, and to offer him preserved, and in summary. I hope I can indicate in several cold and clear sentences the marvelous precision of his voice, in harmony with the chastity of his mind. Here is Mr. Flintlock, exactly as he thinks, and speaks:

"Faith is a totality. Faith is not a partiality. God meant it to be a submission. God never intended it to be a choice. Faith is an inchoative trust. Faith is not an inchoative suspicion. It is a vision, an admiration, a contemplation. It is not an observation, an examination, and a classification. It does not observe everywhere, and see nothing. It sees one thing everywhere it looks. Faith is not to look and keep on looking. Faith is to look—and see."

It never was quite clear to me to what Mr. Flintlock meant to apply this homily. My own urges were to take it as Catholic, and, of course, with a capital *C*. But I am afraid Mr. Flintlock may have uttered it as catholic, with a small *c*. Still, I am not quite sure. There was no interrupting him while he talked. And he refused to give an explanation. So I left him discoursing to himself, and moved on further in the Park.

I had frequently heard of Hoxton, a section of London where folks talk English without the use of consonants. I often meant to go over there; and eventually I did. But long before my visit to Hoxton, I met a man from Hoxton seated in Hyde Park.

I could not believe, when first I was told it, that it was possible to speak English with all consonants cancelled. But Jeff from Hoxton was the boy who could do so, and make no mistake about that. It is hard to describe what one listened to, when he talked. An invertebrate language is marvelously unusual. The best way hurriedly to describe it, is to think of a man with a mouthful of jellyfish, or a bunch of peeled grapes without seeds.

Sentences with nothing but vowels in them are impossible to transliterate, but perhaps I can offer a slight piece of Hoxtonese by an excessive use of *w's.* I give you Jeff saying one of his pieces. A prayer of his, as a piece, will do. And the Our Father was the clearest of all his clouded prayers.

> "Wah Wahwah, woo wah wee Wehweh,
> Wahwoe wee Wye Way . . ."

It sounded to me, for all the world, like the prayer of Jeremias:

> *"A A A, Domine Deus, ecce nescio loqui,*
> *Quia puer ego sum."*

But the prayer of Jeremias was one that was heard. And so Jeff and Jeremias may go together, the babbler in Hoxton and the babbler in Babylon, who both had their way of vowelizing their prayers and uttering them in praise of God.

The London bobby (policeman) is a problem all by himself. In a London street, he looks as cold and mechanical as a traffic light. But in Hyde Park, he looks twice as forbidding. After all, people in London streets are seriously going about their business. But people in Hyde Park are not. Irregular habits in Hyde Park are the regular order of the day.

The London policeman is terribly manly. One wonders if any woman ever spoke to him affectionately. One wonders also how he proposed to the girl who became his wife, unless it was to have held a club above her head and then report her acceptance to headquarters. But I know, and so does everyone with a kind heart, that hidden in the depths of a London policeman, especially the one on a Hyde Park assignment, there are noble longings, that at times become tender, and are haunted by the footsteps of loneliness.

It was in remembrance of one night in Hyde Park, when I watched a London policeman go by, in solicitude and in solitude, that I put him patrolling in the following verse:

When the stars in crowds,
And the moon in her garments of clouds
Come out in the sky,
I

Am the policeman in the park;
When the citizens are sitting or strolling,
And the lovers are patrolling
In the dark.
I make sure
That everything is safe and secure:
That the grass is growing,
And the fountain flowing,
And the breeze, blowing,
And that the trees are covered with bark.
My manner is somewhat distant and severe;
Here and there I make a remark.
I pass the time of day as you would pass the
        time of year,
While the fireflies continue to spark.
With the earth below me,
And the air all around and above me;
With few who personally know me,
And no one to love me,—
I am the policeman in the park.

Speaking of policemen, there is no place in the
world where crime is more difficult to commit than
in London. And this is because of the swiftness and
severity with which crime is detected, sentenced, and
punished. London's laws are so strict, and punishment is so extreme, and judicial sentences so swiftly
made, that a potential criminal does not dare to come
within a mile of the crime he would like to perpe-
trate. I heard Hilaire Belloc once put this most con-

vincingly: "A man is killed in London. A month or two later another man is hanged for the crime. Who is hanged for the crime? The man who committed it? This does not matter to London, as long as 'justice' has been conspicuous, and someone has paid the penalty."

It is for this reason that an afternoon in Hyde Park is likely to put one in the company of dangerous persons, as murderous, we might say, as lions, and as meek, we might put it, as lambs. There are also, doubtless, a number of crazy people among the perpetual sitters and smokers on the benches that are free in Hyde Park.

Strangely enough, the Hyde Park bench-sitter who frightened me most was not a gunman, or a lunatic, or a man bent on some vengeance. He was not even a Communist, or an anarchist, or a member of the Socialist Party. He was a little man, with half-holy eyes, who had news to tell anyone he thought would be glad to hear it. He told it to me, and it scared me so much, I have not yet got over the experience. I remember it fearfully, even as I write.

The little man of whom I speak—who made my heart stop and my eyes bulge in my head—wore no collar, and had no hat. But this was because he was carefree and untidy, and not because he wanted to dress like a desperado. He was also unshaven, and very much unshorn, and looked as though he needed a long soak in a bath. He wore a mustache of the drooping kind.

This little man asked me expectantly if I were what London refers to as an "R.C." When I told him I was, he clapped his hands with delight, and started telling me this story about his daughter:

"Won't you come up to the 'ouse, dear Father, and see us sometime? . . . My missus would be glad to see you.

"We 'ave an only daughter, we 'ave, but she ups and leaves us one day, and goes off to a convent to be a nun. . . .

"I could 'ardly object to that, could I? . . . even though I am 'er father; because, though I 'ave my rights, God 'as 'is rights, and God's rights are greater than mine. . . .

"Our 'ouse, 'owever, was pretty lonely, after our only daughter went away. . . .

"I used to tell the neighbors, when they asked me about 'er, that what she did was go running off with God; and though I 'ad plenty of 'eartaches to go with this, I never 'ad any objections. . . .

"Our daughter writes us a letter, every single week. . . . The missus keeps these letters on the mantel shelf at 'ome, and reads them to me, start and finish, every fortnight. That's all we do by way of diversion, since our daughter went away —is read the letters, sendin' us 'er love, and lettin' us know 'ow 'ard she is prayin' for our salvation. . . .

"What more could a father ask? Or a mother, too, for that matter? The missus and I feel our 'ouse 'as been greatly 'onored. A vocation to religious life is no small thing to get from 'eaven, and we are so glad it was sent to the only one of three of us who was able to respond, and to follow it. . . .

"But even though the missus and I didn't go away ourselves, I still feel we share in our daughter's vocation. My wife feels this in 'er way, and, frankly, I feel it in mine.

"As I said to the missus the other night—and, though she looked surprised, she knew that what I was saying was somehow true—if our daughter is the spouse of 'er Saviour, that makes me the father-in-law of Jesus Christ. . . ."

I felt as though I had been shot in some blasphemous manner. I was almost tempted to deny that I was "what London calls an 'R.C.'" There was no way to answer. And no way to object.

But wisest, it seemed to me, of all of Hyde Park's sit-down philosophers, was Watson, the man who was anxious to put Einstein in his place. Whether or not Einstein made local appearances in London, I do not know. But he is much talked of there.

Einstein's almost-namesake, Epstein (Jacob Epstein) has a sculpture in the Tate Gallery, that would make any man possessed of true Christian sentiment want to draw his dagger, if he had one, and drive it through Epstein's throat. It is a bronze sculpture, purporting to portray the visitation of Our Blessed Lady to the house of her cousin, St. Elizabeth. Our Lady has just been told by the Angel Gabriel the news of the Incarnation, has bowed her head as handmaid of the Lord, and Emmanuel is now in her womb.

Jacob Epstein of London then puts her in motion. The motion itself is an eager one, and so we may understand that the artist admires it as a journey. But the traveler herself is an ugly girl in pigtails, about as much resembling the Queen of Heaven as any of Epstein's thoughts resemble the majestic thoughts of God.

Whether or not Gertrude Stein (another almost-Einstein in name) ever visited London by way of influencing it, I do not know. I suspect she did most of her work in Paris, assisted in her tasks by Alice B. Toklas, and companioned by the proud pity of Pablo Picasso.

Be all this as it may, Watson, the anti-Einstein expert, sits on a bench in Hyde Park, and takes his cracks at Albert, the King in the royal palace of No Dimensions.

Before I come to what Watson has to say about Einstein, there will be no harm in giving what some versifier (whose name I regret I do not remember)

has had to say about Epstein, Stein and Einstein, put
together in a satirical limerick.

Oh, the wonderful family of Stein,
There's Gert, and there's Ep, and there's Ein.
Gert's poems are punk,
Ep's statues are junk,
And no one can understand Ein.

We may now return to our bench-sitting Watson,
on the exclusive subject of Einstein.

Watson uses London's place inclinations, its sense
of concrete things, and its human equations in all
measurements, to settle Einstein's worries about what
space, motion and time may mean. It is Watson's
theory that not only have the philosophers not
cleared up these values by their insolent definitions,
but neither has Einstein by his conceited mathemat-
ics.

"Leave space and motion and time alone," says
Watson. "Or, if you handle them, handle them with
a little human reverence, as shadows of the brightness of God's immensity, power and eternity; and
then you will get out of the notion of space, motion
and time all the realization you ever were entitled
to."

Here is Watson's little lesson on space:

"You may take it," he says, "in scientific measure-
ment, and then it is a foot, or a yard, or a mile. Or,
you may take it," he says, "in an artisan's blueprint,

and it is a room, a house, or a street. If you then want to hand it over to the world at large, it is a town, a district, a country, or a hemisphere. Now, for God's sake," says Watson—to whoever happens to be sitting beside him—"what more does anyone with a brain in his head want to know about space?"

Watson then goes on to the subject of motion.

"If you have a metronome on your piano, and are trying to measure the motion of some musical piece, it is either *lento, moderato,* or *presto.* If you dispense with an instrument, and measure motion by your nerves, it is slow, or medium, or fast. If you give it over to the magnitudes at which men depart from home, then they either go, or travel, or journey, or voyage.

"Time," continues Watson, "is not a bit more difficult to appreciate. When a watch is in your hand, time is a second, or a minute, or an hour. If you left your watch at home, then time is now, or soon, or later. And if you hand it over to calendars, it is a day, or a month, or a year, or a century.

"Now that's all you need," says Watson, "to know about space, and motion, and time. That's all dear Jesus ever gave us in the Gospel. Anything further than this, that Albert Einstein adds, is just a lot of speculative and scientific damn-foolery!"

"Good-bye, Watson," you say, "and thank you."

And, with the look of a humble professor in his eye, Watson's simple reply is, "You're welcome!"

154

Perhaps my readers are now tired, sitting on benches so long. So, let us get up and go over to the "pitches." These are elevated benches on which talkers shout, with official licenses to do so from municipal headquarters.

These outdoor forums, or pitches, are an implicit tribute to the amount of excellent speculative thought London has discovered brewing in Hyde Park. It was precisely because London sensed how much loiterers on benches had to say, that it stood them up, for people to get a look at, and for policemen and inspectors to listen to. London has a way of being very efficiently thoughtful.

One must not imagine that the Speakers' Row in Hyde Park is a place to go for entertainment. No mixture of a law court, a vaudeville house, and a church, in one acre of land, could possibly be called entertainment.

Some of the speakers, of course, have entertaining things to say. I remember one somewhat elderly man, with a cultivated singing voice, advocating the return of old-fashioned love songs, like "When Nellie Was a Lady" and "Let Me Call You Sweetheart." What he was saying was entertaining enough, provided your ear was closed to what a man was shouting on the pitch that was next to his. It was the voice of a wild evangelical, with hatred in his very teeth, clutching a Bible and spitting insult into the face of the most innocent of his listeners!

"You say He's God. I say He's not. Call Him Christ, if you care to. But He's no more God than I am. And if you think I'm not telling you the truth, let God strike me dead this instant. I dare Him to do so."

He then stood in an almost sanctuary silence, for about a minute. And, finding himself still unstruck by the vengeance of God, he added: "You see what I mean?"

The pitch where the Roman Catholic speakers lecture is not the main show in Hyde Park, by any means; but one always finds a good crowd there, consisting of the most serious listeners, the most irrepressible hecklers, and the most potted drunks in the Park.

Introductory information about the purpose of this pitch one can get on the outskirts of the crowd. It is eagerly given by an intellectual girl, with irregularly bobbed hair, and an efficient semimasculine dress, and whom I may call Matilda from Walsingham.

Matilda lets you know, with a polite finger of warning, and in brisk, pleasant tones, that the speakers on the Catholic pitch do not worry about what good they are doing. They leave that to God. They hope for conversions to the Faith. But if conversions are impossible, other benefits may be achieved—like turning a non-Conformist into an Anglican, or bettering a Low Anglican by making him a High one.

In addition to benches and pitches in Hyde Park, there is also an occasional wheel chair. In the Hyde Park of my memories, an old lady in her late seventies has just rolled in. It is beside her wheel chair I am most anxious to sit, and it is she whom I am most anxious to visit. Her name is Alice Wardroper.

I always told Alice Wardroper that she sounded to me like a cowboy's sweetheart. But this was too American for her to appreciate. She told me, however, that her name was originally *Wardrober*. She said her husband's great, great, great, great, great grandfather (I hope I have gone far enough) was a keeper of the wardrobe of King Henry VIII. Dame Alice says she shudders at such family connections. She abhors heretical kings. As heretical, I am sure she dislikes Henry VIII, because she is an ardent Catholic. But as historical, I am not quite so sure she is displeased with her royal connections.

Dame Alice Wardroper is the wife of an officer in the British Army. She was one of those wives who did not go overseas with her husband. She stayed at home, and waited for him, for months, sometimes years, to return. She wrote him letters every week, studied maps to find out where he was, and kept her heart faithful to all his exploits in various army camps—to songs he sang, and the un-English persons

157

he met. She devoured his diaries when he mailed them home for her to read. God sent her one child, in all this married life of separation, and that was a girl named Angela.

Dame Alice Wardroper wore a black ribbon around her throat, and always some lace at the ends of her sleeves. She had cataracts in her eyes. She was also nearly deaf. She had once fallen down a flight of stairs, all by herself, without any husband to protect her. In this frightful accident, she broke her hip; and when it was repaired, one leg was shorter than the other. On one of her shoes she had to wear three or four soles of leather, to keep it on a plane with the other one.

And yet, I can safely say—and hundreds of Alice Wardroper's friends will agree with me—that there never was an old lady in England who better overcame handicaps, and did so with the absolute grace of a girl. Her delicacies and affections—the style she had with which to greet you; the faithful remembrances she kept of the least liking you had in the matter of food or comfort, when you consented to visit her; even the modes with which she managed to put a shawl around her shoulders, or fumbled for her glasses when she was looking for something she had lost—made Alice Wardroper, at seventy-eight, a London girl to remember.

As we sit beside Dame Alice's wheel chair in one of the side paths in Hyde Park, we know at once, from the assurances in her looks, and from the nods she gives in so many directions, that she has friends and admirers and companions, from every age, and walk, and station.

Here is one of Alice Wardroper's admirers coming down the walk. He is a young novelist, named Richard Oke. He likes to haunt Dame Alice, chiefly for the joy of seeing how she listens to whatever he wants to offer her by way of literary amusement. The name Richard Oke is a pseudonym. His real name is Nigel Millet. He is trying hard to write novels. I do not know if he has succeeded, or whether or not he will succeed. But one thing he does successfully, and that is appreciate Dame Alice Wardroper. He knows whatever she is doing or saying is always fit for a paragraph in a book.

Alice Wardroper's slightest exploit is either so charming, so naïve, so pitiful, or so unexpected, that, though consigned, herself, to a life of helplessness, her whole day is one of activity.

When night comes on, Alice Wardroper has to be carried upstairs to her bed. This service her daughter, Angela, now grown-up, is usually allowed to fulfill. But anyone sitting in the Wardroper living room, is always anxious for the privilege.

The nemeses in Alice Wardroper's life are two spinsters who live in the other half of her house. Between her and them is a wall, altogether too thin. Behind this wall, Dame Alice's feminine neighbors are always listening, by way of discovering disturbances they can complain about. Upon this wall they are constantly knocking, to let Alice Wardroper know they have been disturbed. The names of these suspicious sisters are Viola and Veronica Morrison. And Dame Alice's almost constant whisper of warning is:

"*Shhhhhh!* The Morrisons will hear you!"

I do not blame Dame Alice for disliking the unmarried Morrisons. No one can raise a voice in her house, or walk with a heavy step, or make a point in conversation by striking his hand on the table, without their hearing it in the next apartment. And as for loud laughter, they find it insufferable.

When Dame Alice Wardroper has been carried upstairs to bed at night, if she wants anything later on from her daughter, Angela, she never dares call out loud. This would annoy the Morrison Girls, who would pretend they had been wakened from sleep. Dame Alice, therefore, for any assistance she may require late at night, has to give warning notices to the floor below by way of little knocks, and taps, and coughs of every conceivable kind.

I am so glad I have Richard Oke with us, here in Hyde Park at this moment, so that he may tell you, in his own inimitable way, one of Dame Alice's midnight stories.

"This is Richard Oke speaking. Would you like to hear about the weird experience I had at Alice's the other night?

"Angela Wardroper had just carried her mother up to bed. Angela was sitting, reading in the living room. I happened to be walking by the house on one of my late excursions. I saw a light in the Wardroper window. I thought I would go in.

"Angela was so engrossed in her book that she neither heard me come in, nor did she want to bother with conversation. And so I went over and lay down on the sofa, and began reading a book myself.

"The next thing you know, I began to hear—or at least began to think I was hearing—the most minute, infinitesimally small, microscopic little noises it is possible for a human ear to listen to. At first I thought I was imagining things; but after a moment or two I knew I was not. So I summoned up my courage, and spoke to Angela, who, as I say, was engrossed in her book.

" 'Angela,' I said, 'Angela.'

" 'Yes?' said Angela.

" 'Did your parlor mouse, by any chance, hatch today a brood of little mouselings, and are they now trying out their tiny teeth on the furniture?'

" 'Why do you ask that?' said Angela.

" 'Because never in my life have I listened to such incessant, suspicious little sounds as I have been listening to for the past few minutes.'

"Whereupon I got up, and went about examining things in the living room, to see where these naughty little noises might be coming from. I looked behind pictures. I peeked under vases. I lifted up cups. I turned over the corners of tablecovers. I examined the crevices in the chairs, and even poked at pieces of wallpaper loose on the wall; but still no clue. In sheer desperation—and it was getting perilously close to midnight—I opened the door, and went out into the hall. And behold. . . .

"Standing on the top of the stairs was her Ladyship. Dame Alice Wardroper. With a handful of minutiae. Which she was tossing, one by one, down the stairs. First came a machine needle. Then came a paper fastener. Then a linen button. Then a cascara pill. Then half of an aspirin tablet. . . .

" 'What are you doing?' I called up to her. 'What are you doing, Dame Alice? What are you doing, and what do you want?'

" 'I want to attract Angela's attention,' she said.

" 'With the aid of this notion store?'

" 'I don't want to wake the Morrison Sisters,' she whispered loudly. 'But I want Angela to come up, for something that I need.'

"Just at this moment, the bell in a nearby church-tower started striking the hour of midnight. And oh! I *do* tell you, it is a terrifying thing, at the dead hour of midnight, to hear a linen button, or an aspirin tablet, come bouncing down the stairs; or to listen to a cascara pill go crashing into the wall.

"'You want to attract your daughter's attention?' I called to Dame Alice.

"'Yes!' she whispered in a shriek.

"'With all these picayune trinkets?' I replied.

"'Yes!' she shrieked once again.

"'Oh! I see!' said I, 'I get the idea. You drop a bread crumb, and your daughter comes!'"

I do not know what became of this Richard Oke. But I do know what became of Alice Wardroper. She died. And I am sure that my remembrance of her, now written, will remind her in Heaven what I once promised her on earth. And that was, that I never would forget her.

And as I bid farewell to Hyde Park, whose benches, pitches, and even wheel chairs, have given me such pleasure and delight, I trust I will be pardoned for making my next enterprise—finding what has emptied the pews in the London churches.

VIII

LONDON PREACHERS

On the subject of London preachers, perhaps we ought to begin with the most worked preacher London has known in the past century. He is the Very Rev. W. R. Inge, K.C.V.O., F.B.A., D.D., the Dean of St. Paul's. Dean Inge is over ninety years of age, and has preached in every English cathedral except Southwell.

When Dean Inge is talking in St. Paul's Cathedral, it is hard to know whether he is preaching, lecturing, or giving an address. So perhaps we ought to add, in addition to his acknowledged work in the pulpit, some of his platform work, as well. He has given the Gifford Lectures, the Paddock Lectures in America, the Romanes and Herbert Spencer Lectures in Oxford, the Hulsean and Rede Lectures at Cambridge, the Hibbert Lectures, the Jowett Lectures, the Liverpool Lecture, the Warburton Lectures, the Galton Lecture, and two or three at the London hospitals. Many more lectures he could have had if he were willing to travel far enough. Australia he declined with regret. It would have taken him too long from London. He also declined Germany.

In addition to his sermons and lectures, Dean Inge has given innumerable addresses, everywhere. Again, his addresses are indiscernible, even by the most astute listener, from his work on the platform or in the pulpit. He has given addresses in America twice, in Sweden, Norway, Holland, Switzerland, and Greece.

To his work of preaching, lecturing and addressing, we perhaps ought to add, in all fairness, some of Dean Inge's other clerical employment. Besides being the Dean of St. Paul's, he has been President of the Modern Churchmen's Union, of the Clergy Home Mission Union, and of the Religious Thought Society, of which he is an assistant founder.

If we were to add to that, the clubs to which Dean Inge has belonged, including the Hellenic Travelers' Club, the London Clerical and Medical Committee, the Guild of Freemen, the Birth-Rate Commission, the International Medical Congress, the Middlesex Hospital Associates, the Women's Diocesan Association, the Ecclesiastical Commission

Committee, the Clergy Home Mission Union, the Musicians' Company, and the Church Family Newspaper Editors;—to say nothing of innumerable others I cannot recall—it is no wonder that Dean Inge has secured for himself, among other reputations, that of being the outstanding Neo-Platonist of our day. He is a new version of Plato's Universal Man.

It is also no wonder that he got gloomy, being so much on the go. Seated at any one dinner table, his thought had to be: Where do I eat next? Whom do I meet next? Whom do I greet next? Where do I move my feet next? It is hard not to be depressed, dressed up in black, while fulfilling such incessant obligations.

Dean Inge admits that he dined out at night, never less than two or three times a week, which is well over a hundred nights a year, and practically one night out of three. And this is not counting luncheons, which occurred in the middle of the day. Nor teas, every afternoon. There was even an occasional breakfast, thrown in here and there, in the morning.

Perhaps the next thing we ought to ask about Dean Inge is this: What did he say when he preached? My answers are going to be taken either from his sermons, lectures, addresses, conferences, or just plain chats. Oh yes, I forgot—or from his diaries. Because Dean Inge, whenever he was left alone, was always preaching to himself.

Dean Inge dressed always in somber black, with clerical collar, and—until a few years ago—in gaiters. He was what is known in London as a Low Church Anglican. But he travelled only in the highest society.

Either one must call everything Dean Inge did preaching, or else it is wrong to call that preaching which he did with vestments on in the pulpit. And let no one think, for all that he claimed to be a retiring man, that he has not made a lasting public impression on London.

Dean Inge is London's quintessential clergyman. He is that to which all London beliefs are pointing whenever they imply "the church," "a cleric," or "the cloth." If Dean Inge did not exist, London would have had to invent him. London needs only to say "the gloomy Dean." All the rest of its clergy are then brushed aside, eliminated, pushed out of the picture, no matter how sad-faced or pious or jurisdictional they may look.

Being a Low Anglican and not a High one; being a Protestant and not a Catholic; being a practical man and not a mystic; being an idealist in thought and not a realist; being a realist in history and not an idealist; being a cleric and not a layman; being a married man and not a monk; being, if somewhat somber, always social; and although set apart for the sanctuary, yet seething therein with secular notions, —Dean Inge manages to spot himself a friend or defender in every area of public life. Somebody always has some reason for liking him, and for saying that he is not as bad as he is cracked up to be. The most frequent reference one hears made of Dean Inge is: At least you've got to admit that the Dean was on the right side of this controversy . . . that discussion . . . this debate . . . that disclaimer . . . this doubt . . . or that decision.

Dean W. R. Inge and Lord Bertrand Russell are exactly the theologian and the philosopher the British Empire requires, so as to leave it unembarrassed in its pursuits. Inge gives London gloomy theology; Russell gives it the philosophy of despair. After thinking in the territory of these two, anything is a relief, even British Empire annoyances: high taxes, low wages, bad food.

Dean Inge believes in the salvation of the precious few. He endeavors to show charity towards this arrangement by taking it gloomily. Lord Bertrand Russell believes in the damnation of the unprecious everybody, and maintains we should look on this with satisfaction. Inge and Russell often have it out together, and pretend to be intellectual enemies. When Bertrand Russell makes a statement like this:

"Only on the firm foundation of unyielding despair can the soul's habitation henceforth be safely built,"

Dean Inge dandles the statement with a great deal of reflection. He hopes he can ultimately settle it serenely by his distinction between the ideal and the real order.

Dean Inge is a Protestant divine who thinks damnation is ideal, as long as it occurs in the ideal order, which is to say, the order to which he does not belong. Bertrand Russell is an heretical atheist who thinks his own damnation, of which he is certain (and so am I) is the presage of damnation for all, and is desirable because there is no escape from it.

I may now let Dean Inge tell a little of his own story. He is most anxious to.

His humility:

"I have no social gifts. I have inherited from my mother's family, the Churton's, the faculty of being silent in several languages. I have been further handicapped by slowly increasing deafness, and by a ridiculous inability to remember faces. I have failed to recognize at least three duchesses, and a score of less exalted people."

Some thoughts, while listening to the choir of St. Paul's:

"I can and do pray when I 'enter into my chamber and shut the door'; but in the midst of howling and caterwauling, I cannot."

" 'Melodies heard are sweet, but those un-heard are sweeter.' Quite right, John Keats; they are."

" 'Music hath charms to soothe the savage beast.' It has the opposite effect on me, who am not a savage."

"If I believed that I shall listen through all eternity to the seraphim blowing their loud, up-lifted trumpets, it would almost deter me from the practice of virtue."

"They turned the Nicene Creed into an an-them; before the end, I had ceased to believe anything."

" 'Use not vain repetition.' For ten minutes to-day the choir repeated the words, 'I wrestle and pray.' "

"Are we quite sure that the Deity enjoys being serenaded?"

Mutual admiration:

"Bernard Shaw, while wholly disagreeing with me in politics, speaks of me as, 'our great Dean,' 'our most extraordinary writer, and in some respects our most extraordinary man.' "

"Bernard Shaw is a good man, and a great man, and he is kind enough to wish to be our friend."

Thoughts on Catholic Saints:

"After the Reformation the Catholic Church became narrower, and no longer produced men of genius, like Augustine, or even Thomas Aquinas. Its most outstanding figures are, Ignatius of Loyola and Alfonso of Liguori, in whom 'vulgar Catholicism' overwhelms the mystical and evangelical elements of Christianity."

The Church of England:

"The question, 'What does the Church of England stand for?' must, of course, be answered. It can be answered only by considering what it has stood for since the Reformation and before it. It has been . . . the church of the English people. This is the principle upon which Hooker most insists. 'There is not any man of the Church of England but the same man is also a member of the Commonwealth; nor any man a member of the Commonwealth, who is not also (a member) of the Church of England.' "

The Chosen People:

"We need a Bible of the English race, which shall be hardly less sacred to each succeeding generation of young Britons than the Old Tes-

171

tament is to the Jews. England ought to be, and may be, the spiritual home of one-quarter of the human race, for ages after our task as a World-Power shall have been brought to a successful issue, and after we in this little island have accepted the position of mother to nations greater than ourselves."

On the death of his daughter, Margaret Paula:

"It has been my strange privilege, as I believe, to have been the father of one of God's saints, a character as pure and beautiful as many which are recorded in the Church's Role of Honor."

I am sorry, but I think this is all I have to say on the subject of Dean Inge of St. Paul's. It pleases me to think he had a daughter whom he loved. It pleases me even more to notice (which I think escaped his own notice) that the highest tribute he could pay to her was to put her on the Role of Honor of the Church which he despises. It grieves me to think that she was not canonized by more infallible authority.

Carl Sandburg, a mid-western American poet, who called his native habitat "Hog-Butcher for the World," and expected Chicago schoolchildren to be pleased, endeavored once to put a fog into verse. He called it a little cat.

The fog comes
on little cat feet.
It sits looking
over harbor and city
on silent haunches
and then moves on.

The fog comes on little cat feet. Does it? I agree
it comes softly and silently, but its own softness and
silence are all too evident to me without my needing
to have them emphasized in terms of the softness
and silence of something not in the least more soft
or more silent. What good does it do to say of a ball
that it is as round as an orange, or of a piece of
coal that it is as black as a crow? Supposing I were
to write Sandburg's poem emphasizing the resemblances between a little cat and a big fog?

The little cat creeps into the room
as silent as a big fog.
Softly it fills my chamber
and sits watching a tiny mouse
scampering towards a hole
which despite the presence of the cat-like fog
has not become invisible.

Perhaps we now understand why the London poets
left the theme of fog alone.

Perhaps we also can understand why a young Indian girl, Lyra Ribeiro, after a taste of America's
proletarian poets from places like Chicago, should

innocently reply from an undemocratic place like
Goa:

> To root and star
> To leaf and stone
> To little things that are
>> Alone,
> To snail and moth
> And such-like, each,
> God spared the greater loneliness
>> Of speech.

To be foggy on the subject of fog, is bad enough;
but what shall we say of being foggy on the subject
of Faith?

One might think that because Archbishop William
Temple, the late Archbishop of Canterbury, was an
Anglican on a higher plane than Dean Inge, that he
would be definite about things that are doctrinal,
authoritative about them, and occasionally apostolic.
He was not. Not only did he lack Dean Inge's clear
powers of affirmation, he actually cast doubts on
Faith itself.

Many of the Archbishop of Canterbury's sermons disregarded entirely the facts of Faith. They
were concerned only with Faith as a function. It can
be truly said of him, no matter how shocking it
sounds—that he did not believe in God. He believed
in belief.

Here are a few of Dr. Temple's statements taken from a sermon he delivered in a Church at Oxford, when he was the Archbishop of York, and before his government appointment to be the Archbishop of Canterbury. And here are a few of the replies I made to them, at a lecture delivered before the Nicene Society of Oxford, in the year 1931. The lecture was presided over by Dr. S. Vernon Bartlett, a Non-Conformist, and President of Manchester College.

The Archbishop of York:

Faith in God is precisely an hypothesis that the one principle which is capable of offering a final explanation of the universe does, in fact, explain it.

Reply:

This means that we take a chance on the chance that there may be a God.

The Archbishop of York:

For us, finite beings in this world, that which calls forth our noblest capacities is always a hazard of some kind, never a certainty.

Reply:

I always thought a hazard involved the difficult attainment of something you knew was there to attain. What would you think of asking

175

me to bet my money on an imaginary race horse
in the hope that he would spring into existence
in time to run in the race?

The Archbishop of York:

To adapt our lives with caution, to follow established certainties, is not in the least noble or
heroic; it is merely sensible.

Reply:

What superiority has religion over any other
form of human activity in tempting us to em-
brace uncertainty?

The Archbishop of York:

Faith is something nobler in its own kind than
certainty.

Reply:

Possibly there is an ignorance in its own kind
nobler than knowledge; a darkness nobler than
light; a Blessed Ignorance and a Beatific Darkness, so to speak.

The Archbishop of York:

There used to be in this country a study called
'Mods,' or formal logic, which divided the processes by which men think when in pursuit of
truth, into deductive and inductive. If God exists,

176

then you may draw deductions from His nature, but from the very nature of deduction itself, you cannot reach Him by means of it. Nor can you hope to get there by induction, by looking about in the world for a variety of events which you cannot explain any other way. You could never say there was one cause which explained them all; you could never, therefore, reach God.

Reply:

The existence of a sole cause of the universe is proved by both processes of thought, induction and deduction, employed not simultaneously, but successively.

Our third London preacher is a Catholic priest. He comes from a family in which five daughters were nuns, and six sons were priests. Three of them became Bishops, and one of them was made a Cardinal.

Our third London preacher is the magnanimous, broad-gestured, handsome, kindly-eyed, Father Bernard Vaughan. He was a younger brother of Herbert Cardinal Vaughan, the third Archbishop of Westminster, and who built Westminster Cathedral.

Father Bernard Vaughan had the first requisite for an impressive preacher; he was himself impressive. At Holy Name Church, in Manchester, where he was stationed for a time, he had charge of the building of a pulpit. He designed it for a great preacher's needs. One ascended it, not by a sudden and clumsy stair, but by a gradual ramp, as though floating up a hill. Father Vaughan's pulpit was commodious, and was constructed of marble and imperishable wood. Behind where the preacher stood was a beautiful concave shell. It was calculated to show the preacher off, itemized to perfection. I myself preached in this pulpit for fifteen consecutive nights; and felt totally unworthy of it, entering and leaving.

Though Father Bernard Vaughan's congregations were mostly London's high society, he made efforts to be evangelical according to the Gospel's humble prescriptions. He went out into the London lanes, ringing a bell and summoning the crowds to hear him speaking on the street-corner. Father Vaughan was a man of God who could dine with kings, and still not lose the common touch.

And dine with kings he did. King Edward VII of England was constantly inviting him to Buckingham Palace to dinner. There was, in the royal dining-room, a life-size picture of King Henry VIII.

"What would you do," Father Vaughan was asked, "if Henry VIII stepped out of that picture?"

"I would ask the ladies to leave the room," he said.

Great numbers of people in Mayfair, knighted, or wealthy, or both, came to hear a course of sermons given by Father Vaughan, entitled "The Sins of Society." The pews at these fashionable sermons were kept open for their pew-holders, up until five minutes before sermon time. After that, anyone standing at the door could rush in and take an empty place.

One night, Lady Bedingfeld came late for one of these sermons. Lady Bedingfeld was a tall, London beauty, of conspicuous manner and voice. The church was packed. The empty places in all the pews, including her own, had been filled. Father Vaughan was ready to come out into the pulpit, dressed in his black silk cassock.

It was then that Lady Bedingfeld walked, un-ushered, down the middle aisle, and in view of, and in hearing of all, was heard to say, to a young shirt-waist seller sitting in her place, "I beg your pardon, are you Lady Bedingfeld?"

"No, ma'am."

"Well, I am; and that's her seat."

Surely, a more brilliant change of personal pronoun has never been recorded.

It was interesting to watch Father Vaughan come out to preach at Mass. He loved altar boys. He delighted in seeing droves of them walk ahead of him in white surplices and dark cassocks, with folded hands and lowered eyes. Father Vaughan never hurried his acolytes.

Father Vaughan particularly liked to wear a cape in the sanctuary, and then ceremoniously to take it off; and to hand it, with a bow of almost personal regard, to whoever took charge of it while he was busy in the pulpit.

Father Vaughan's prayer at the foot of the altar, antecedent to his sermon, he never hurried, nor did he move towards the pulpit quickly. He approached it in slow strides. And when he had finally reached and ascended it, he stood there, tall and erect, for what always seemed like the major part of a minute. He gave the congregation a good long gaze of recognition, and, turning sideways, was handsome in profile; and then, front forward he turned once more. And in the midst of slow, deliberate and majestic breathing, with beautiful intonation and superb reverence, he both made and spoke the Sign of the Cross.

Father Vaughan's sermons were enormously pleasing. His patterns of thought were aristocratic, simple, benignant, and clear. Here is a fashion in which he might begin:

"My dear Brethren: Life may be compared to a game of chess. In a game of chess there are various wooden pieces, the King, the Queen, the Knights, the Bishops, the Castles, and the Pawns. These are the parts these pieces play, while the game of chess is going on.

"The Pawns are the smallest of the pieces, and they move forward only one space at a time. By special privilege, they may move two. The

Castles must move in squares; the Knights must move in angles; and the Bishops diagonally.

"Last of all, we come to the King and the Queen. The King and Queen may move in any direction; the Queen in lengthy, royal excursions; the King in majestic, slow ones.

"Before the game of chess is over, some inconspicuous Pawn may turn out to be the most valiant defender of the King, and on this otherwise unimportant piece, victory may depend. And so it is in life.

"Life is a game of chess. It is most like it when the game is ended; for then it is when all the pieces, independent of their former dignities and prerogatives, are packed in the same little box, King and Queen, Bishop and Pawn, and put away on the shelf."

When Father Bernard Vaughan had finished his sermon, he walked back into the sacristy with the same regal air with which he had come out of it. He had that quality which Willa Cather once praised in a good priest. He had "beautiful manners with himself even when he was alone."

One day Father Vaughan was in a small town in Lancashire, called Wigan. He was leaving the town, and was standing in the railroad station awaiting the train, which was late. He went up to the baggageman, piling trunks, and said:

"What is the name of this place?"

"Wigan."

Father Vaughan paced up and down the platform a few more times.

"What did you say the name of this place was?" he said again to the man.

"WIGAN!" the fellow shouted. "Look at that sign, starin' you in the face!"

Again Father Vaughan, after a few more excursions up and down the platform, and because there was still no train arriving, went up once more to the same employee.

"I have a dreadfully bad memory," he said. "What is the name of this place?"

"How did you get here if you didn't know what the name of it was?" the man shrieked, walking away from him.

The train finally arrived. Father Vaughan boarded the train and entered one of the compartments. He sat down with a large, audible sigh.

"Oh!" he said. "Oh! I am so glad to get out of this place. I have never met such uncivil people. They are so discourteous, so impolite."

"I don't agree with you, Reverend," said one of the other passengers in the compartment, putting down his morning paper. "Lancashire folk are well known for being courteous and polite, particularly the folk from Wigan."

182

"Well, then, let us see," said Father Vaughan, as he opened the train window and beckoned to the baggage-man.

"Will you please tell me what is the name of this place?"

"Will you go to *hell!*" the fellow replied.

"Do you see what I mean?" said Father Vaughan, closing the window.

Father Vaughan preached in many other cities besides London and Manchester. Indeed, he preached in many other countries besides England. I heard him preach in Boston. The Mikado of Japan listened to him preach, in Tokyo.

At the end of one of Father Vaughan's sermons, on Heaven, he started perorating as he left the pulpit. "To Heaven!" he said, as he went down step after step. "To Heaven!" he repeated, as he entered the sanctuary and closed the gate. . . . "To Heaven!" he cried, as he genuflected, and started to go out—the wrong sanctuary door.

"To Heaven!" he shouted, as he put his hand on the door-knob, and prepared to turn it and disappear; only to find that the door was locked.

But Father Vaughan was not you or I left in such a predicament. "To Heaven!" he kept on shouting trustfully, until he found the right door. And out that door he went.

There was one trait especially which Father Vaughan possessed, and which I should like to mention before I point out his deficiencies. It was the trait of being a Catholic "to the manner born," and as one is so born, in England. There were no inferiority signals or cultural omissions in his style. He did not have the awkward manners of present-day London apologizers for the Faith.

Father Bernard Vaughan was not in the tradition of the Newman school of preachers. These preachers like to carry written sermons into the pulpit, and then half recite, half read them. Father Vaughan was never a lecturer at the lectern, nor a pulpit pedagogue. He was first, last, and always, a preacher. Those who could not match him at excellence in this, endeavored to depreciate him, and, indeed, through him, pulpit oratory itself.

Father Vaughan always talked in the pulpit in the tones in which he prayed. But the topics of his talks often lacked the tone of his prayers. Here was one of his prayers—a Christmas message which appeared in print:

"Dearest Jesus, on this Gift-giving Day, I offer myself with all that I am and have in life and in death to be entirely Thine. I give Thee my work—do Thou give me rest. I give Thee my sorrows—do Thou give me support. I give Thee my trials—do Thou give me triumph. I give Thee time—do Thou give me Eternity."

184

But all too often, when speaking in public, he tried to offer England a sociological Jesus, instead of the Jesus Who died to save our souls. He made Our Lord the ardent supporter—almost contributor —to all sorts of uplift enterprises, for better food, better living quarters, better hospital care. Here is how he spoke in the pulpit in behalf of a collection for a hospital in Aberdeen.

"If Our Lord were here today pleading for the object for which I am standing in this pulpit, you would see tears upon His cheeks! I think you would."

As a Catholic in the pulpit, Father Vaughan was edifying. As an apostle in the pulpit, he was not always satisfactory.

Father Vaughan did have, as the fruit of his personal apostolate, one notable victory. I shall mention it at the end of this chapter. But instead of a hidden victory, which it was, it should have been a glorious one, set on the summit of a hill, like a city shining in the sun; as a crown on the brow of a King, blazing with light for the astonishment of the world, and for a testimonial to the Kingdom of Heaven.

Over-explanations always displease an Englishman. Eloquence for its own sake is something of an over-explanation, and this is probably why the English are prone to dislike it. But eloquence for God's sake is a requirement that makes no allowances for tastes.

When an Englishman sees a point, he nods. This is a signal for the one who is talking to retire. Yes, even to retire from a pulpit in case the nodding has occurred in a church. For the first time in England since the Sixteenth Century, Father Vaughan made congregations nod from incipient appreciation and deep delight; not, as had been their custom, from incipient slumber and profound sleep. Father Vaughan rid English churches of their sleepers and sleepy sermons. This is my praise of him. But his clarion call, waking Catholics up, did not always let them know what they were waking up to. And this is my criticism.

All utterance in a Catholic pulpit must be pointed to one end: the salvation of souls. There never has been an English saint whose teaching on the subject of salvation has not been as clear and unequivocal as the discourse of Christ to His twelve Apostles.

Father Bernard Vaughan taught with power, according to Christ's command, when He said, "All power is given to Me in Heaven and on earth. Going, therefore, teach . . ." John Henry Newman taught without power, and was a scandal, at least to Our Lord's little ones. I wish, however, that Father Vaughan had added to his power and to the generosities of his heart, the concreteness and the chastity of the Word of God.

Of these two, Newman and Vaughan, give me Vaughan any day. A man may have enthusiasm without Christian truth, but no man can have Christian truth without enthusiasm. Out of the abundance of the heart, the mouth speaketh. Not out of the cautiousness of the mind.

When England forsook the dramatic values of Revealed Truth, its preachers became dry as dust. Its congregations then turned to drama in works of fiction. Chaucer, through fiction, had converted the Cathedral of Canterbury into a Tale, and stopped it from being the Holy Cupboard of the Bread of Life. Geoffrey Chaucer died, beseeching Jesus Christ to forgive him his sins. And I am not a bit surprised.

Jesus Christ was not mystery and mist. He was mystery and vision, in the same adorational thought. Jesus shed His blood for us, and expects us to want to shed our blood for Him. After a sermon by Father Vaughan, one never thought of shedding one's blood for Jesus, but only of paying commemorative respects to those who had done so. But English blood must go on being shed for Jesus, as long as England remains a child (not a mother, Dean Inge!) among the islands of the world, and as long as London is a place.

One night, at the end of a touching sermon, Father Vaughan spoke a phrase which the London liberals did not take to. I myself heard several priests apologize for this phrase, when the story was being told me. It was what they called, "Father Vaughan's overdoing it a bit; meaning well, of course, but unfortunately going too far."

Father Vaughan was talking about the God Who became little enough to be lullabied in Bethlehem. He was trying to put tenderness and adoration into the hearts of his listeners by asking them to remember that God was a Baby. He told them to close their eyes, and listen to the Blessed Mother of Jesus whispering Good-night to Eternal Light as it started to fall asleep.

He urged them to thank Mary for the flesh and blood she gave to Jesus. This Flesh and Blood, he said, transformed into the Bread of Life, transforms us, when we partake of it, into Mary's own children. He said that sometimes at night, Mary might forget which baby she was rocking to sleep—Jesus of Nazareth, or some little London boy or girl.

And with his hand extended high in the sky, and with the pulpit-light shining on his face, and with the church walls echoing his triumphant tones, he made this apostrophe to the Queen of Heaven. He called her:

188

"Oh! *darling* Mother of God!"

And now—as we say in America—comes the pay-off on Father Vaughan.

It is the law of the land in England, and the law of the English Church, that when the King is dying the last clergyman who may see him must be the Archbishop of Canterbury. After the Archbishop of Canterbury's visit to a dying King, no other clergyman is admitted to the royal bedchamber.

The last clergyman who entered the bedroom of King Edward VII, when he was dying, was not the Archbishop of Canterbury. It was Father Bernard Vaughan. And after he came out, no other clergyman went in.

"How did things go," Father Vaughan was asked, concerning the last hours of King Edward VII.

"Everything was quite satisfactory," was all that Father Vaughan ever consented to answer.

But anyone who knows a Catholic priest, knows that there may be great depths in such a reply, without the violation of any secret.

The text of London Is A Place is
set in Linotype Caslon, and the running titles and introductory pages in
Linotype Granjon.